TURN

AND

BURN

A FIGHTER PILOT'S MEMORIES AND CONFESSIONS

Darrell J. Ahrens
Lt. Col. USAF(ret.)
Call Sign: "Curly"

"Turn and burn" is fighter pilot jargon that refers to flying the jet to the edge of its performance capability, and even beyond, with speeds ranging from the stall to the supersonic, with engine afterburner roaring at full power, with gut-wrenching high G forces maneuvering, with the aircraft enveloped in the condensation that accompanies those G forces. In other words, it refers to the most violent flying, with both the jet and the pilot operating at maximum testosterone levels.

REVIEWS

The title of this book, *Turn and Burn*, is a perfect introduction into the book contents, the world of fighter pilots, and the goals of aerospace engineers serving the military. My career as a Program Manager in aerospace engineering and the highly confidential development of military aircraft helped me appreciate the experiences shared by Lt. Col. Darrell J. Ahrens. The book is an easy read for an engineer and an eye-opener into the challenges faced by fighter pilots and their ability to solve problems creatively. The story follows experiences as opposed to time but that keeps the reader intrigued. Readers will obtain thought-provoking insight into the military, pilot discernment, and the courage they have every time they fly.

~ Bruce Wright, Father of the F22 Raptor,
RQ-170 (Beast of Kandahar), Author and Lecturer

"I devoured this book in one day. I found it a fascinating story about all the adventures and travails of an Air Force pilot, starting from his first solo through his very last flight. As a former Marine Corps Aviation Cadet (which the author Ahrens almost became), I related to every one of his exciting stories. I wish he had used more dates so I could know when our paths crossed...his paths very high, mine, as a Marine Corps helicopter pilot, low, but nevertheless intersecting."

~ Bill Collier (USMCR), Author of
The Adventures of a Helicopter Pilot and *Air America*

"*Turn and Burn* presents a well-written, modestly understated, insight into the mind and personality of a fighter pilot, in peace and war, facing challenge and danger with inner calm and grace. The author chronologically inter-leaves chapters of peacetime experiences with those flying combat missions during the Vietnam War, which help the reader capture the measure of the man over a span of years and circumstance. And I could relate. I was a career Army officer. I "knew" Bitburg, Germany, where Ahrens was based during the Cold War. And I fought The Vietnam War on the ground, often the recipient of the close air support from F-4s and F-105s that LT. COL. Ahrens flew, and which often swayed the fight in our favor, and helped bring us home, alive. I particularly enjoyed his chapter on his reflections of the war, having come to the same core conclusions when I indulged in such reflection. Ahrens motivation for writing his book was the preservation of family history. He accomplishes that, and much more. He provides the reader with a rare view of the psychology and culture of those who fly, serve our nation, and who conquer fear and danger."

~ Richard Kurtz, Author of *Then a Soldier*

"This excellent book is firmly in the "there I was..." school of military memoirs. Lt/Col Ahrens describes in vivid detail his life, and almost his death, as a fighter pilot with the United States Air Force including the path he took to hold such a position. He flew the fast jets, the best we had at the time, and flew them well. Written in the first person, the book puts the reader in the cockpit with all the danger, excitement, and stress that entails. Climb aboard, strap in, tighten your lap belt, lock your shoulder harness, and check six with Darrell Ahrens, fighter pilot."

~ Ed Cobleigh, Bestselling author of numerous books including
War For the Hell of It: A Fighter Pilot's View of Vietnam

"Author Darrell J. Ahrens earned his degrees from Chapman University, Boston University, and Fuller Theological Seminary and has served as a US Marine, Air Force fighter pilot and operations staff officer, a high school teacher and a pastor! He bonds all of these experiences in this interesting and involving memoir, sharing his experiences as a fighter pilot so vividly that reading the book offers the sense of being his co-pilot!

The multifaceted experiences of Ahrens' fighter pilot history are especially memorable to those of us who also served in the military in the Vietnam War: battles in the air and on land were related, and the author makes them visual and palpable. On that level alone the book is an exciting reading experience. But the lasting impact is the manner in which he extends his memories into some very solid observations about the mechanics of war, the state of education, the need for faith, and the importance of sharing a life as an invitation for introspection. Adding photographs and color emblems that denote periods of time add greatly to the ambience of this impressive chronicle. Highly recommended for a very broad audience."

~ Grady Harp, Amazon Top Reviewer

"Lt Col Ahrens writes a fascinating collection of vignettes here to provide an interesting perspective on not only the combat sorties of a Vietnam Era pilot but many of the less well recorded training and non-combat missions. Lt Col Ahrens demonstrates a clear and unwavering faith as a thread which ties his stories and journeys together which, although not my own Christian interpretation of gospel, I can respect how it grounds his journey.

Written in an easygoing style, Ahrens provides enough technical details in his recollections to establish his bona fides, but doesn't go beyond that to confuse or bore the lay reader. His choice to present the book as a collection of vignettes makes this an enjoyable read, almost conversational, and you can almost hear his voice in your head as if this is an armchair conversation of his recollections.

Overall a very digestible and interesting read that should be considered by both Air Force and Vietnam buffs for providing a different perspective than many other combat forward works out there."

~ Michael

"As Vietnam era veteran, I enjoyed reading about Lt. Col. Ahrens adventures, misadventures, and reflections on his military career. It was like "old home week" as we say in Army. Veterans from the 60s, 70s and even 80s will enjoy this book because his experiences, insights and opinions will likely align with your own. Air Force fliers of that era will probably like it even more.

He shares combat experiences with the reverence and humility of a true warrior. The fun and camaraderie we experience when we serve is there alongside the deep respect for our fallen. He touches on politics and the warrior viewpoint. He is no radical but shares his solid Christian and American values.

'The cockpit of a fighter aircraft,' he said, "is a place of self-discovery where one is faced with the stark reality of one's capabilities and limitations." He was forthcoming on both. Although, Lt. Col Aherns wrote these recollections for his grandchildren, I felt privileged to share them."

~ Donna Woodward

"The book was written with humor, humility, truthfulness, and wisdom. Ahrens was a Marine who then entered the Air Force to become an exceptional fighter pilot. He shared his mishaps and mistakes, and he learned from those to excel at flying. Moving from a chapter on learning to fly each fighter jet to a chapter on being a fighter pilot in the war in Vietnam eased me into the culture of fighter pilots. He was always willing to share about the different countries in which he was stationed.

I loved his simple way of telling his story and I, at times, felt as if I was one of his kids, learning to know his history, his heart, and his passion. For a fighter pilot, he was just so down to earth in his story-telling."

~ Lynnette Goebel

"As a 'Cold War' Army veteran and certified military history nut, I devour a good military read. I truly enjoyed reading this first-person account of an honorable military pilot. His easy, personable writing style had me joining him in the cockpit... longing for that feeling of power and elation. I grew up with most of the jets mentioned in this book and had the honor of sitting in the WSO seat of a F4 at Andrews where my Uncle worked maintenance. I fondly recall them all as beautiful birds of prey. I can relate to experiencing foreign cultures, having served in Italy and traveling Europe and Turkey. As the author says, "you need to go". I can also relate to Faith. God has been there for me so many times because He had a better plan. Read the book and prepare to slip the surly bonds of earth. Salute LTC!"

~ Bill

"Turn and Burn by Darrell Ahrens is a must read for those of us who appreciate military history, technology and combat experiences. Ahren's style is engaging and conversational. The author, like most true heros, projects a strong sense of integrity, humility and introspection. Unlike many works within this genre, the author minimizes combat drama. Although this book provides plenty of colorful action, the story is predominantly an inspirational journey of a young boy's life long aspiration to become a fighter pilot. The focus is on the chronology of trials, sacrifices and accomplishments along the way. The first ninety percent of this book is clearly written for those of us who love this genre. The last ten percent is a must read for everyone who are concerned for the future of The United States of America."

~ Daniel

★★★★★

"I have read numerous books within this specific genre and to the best of my recollection found this book to be one of my favorites. I felt that the method the author used to "break-up" his life and career path with the insertion of actual combat experience and other flying experiences made the book more interesting and held my attention better than the basic "step-by-step" progress through life used by many authors. As a retired member of the U.S. Navy within a couple of years of his period of service somewhat reminiscent of some of my experiences in the area of military "policies" as an enlisted member; needless to say though not to the same degree of possible consequences. Since I agree totally with his comments in the Chapter *Thoughts and Comments on War*, I definitely found it refreshing."

~ Ernest

DEDICATION

To my wife Louise who stayed the course during the demands of her husband's military flying career when many other wives bailed out of their marriages.

My love forever.

TURN AND BURN: A Fighter Pilot's Memories and Confessions

Copyright © 2020 by Darrell J. Ahrens

Published by Wise Media Group (Morro Bay, CA)
For rights, media & contact visit **WiseMediaGroup.com/darrell**

ISBN 978-1629671871 (Paperback)
ISBN 978-1629671888 (Hardcover)
Library of Congress Control Number: 2020916250

Also available in Audiobook

Project Managed with AuthorDock, produced by Brian Schwartz.

Scripture quotations from *The Authorized King James Version (AKJV)*. Rights in the Authorized Version in the United Kingdom are vested in the Crown. Reproduced by permission of the Crown's patentee, Cambridge University Press.

Rev 2.23

TABLE OF CONTENTS

THE DREAM

An old ramshackle house littered with model airplanes in
  a small midwestern town where kids could run free,
  explore and imagine is where the dream began;

I remember that, and what fun it truly was.
  the old chicken coop behind the house with a high roof
  from which I jumped with a parachute made of a bedsheet
  because I wanted to experience flight;

I remember that, and how badly it hurt when I landed.
  the countless times I looked to the sky at the approaching
  sound and searched intently until flash of sun on metal
  drew my gaze, and a seven year- old marveled at the
  wonder of it and dreamed that one day he would do that.

I remember that as if it were yesterday.

Throughout the years that haunting dream was a constant
  companion, so real yet veiled; so close yet distant;
  reachable yet unreachable; hope becoming desire, desire
  becoming obsession, and faith, always faith that the gift
  would be given.

Oh yes, I remember that!

I remember the day the dream became reality, hope
  fulfilled, the unreachable reached, when flesh and
  metal burst through hallowed portals of sky and wind
  and cloud, and wheeled and soared in beauty
  indescribable, wild and free.

I remember days and years that followed, delight and
  ecstasy, fear and terror, joy and sorrow, laughter and
  tears, when death hovered close but life was truly lived;

13

*and always the intensity, the adventure, the wonder of
it all, going where few go, doing what few do, seeing
what few see.*

*I remember too when it ended, as if awakening from a dream
that one desperately holds onto; unwilling to leave that
which demanded so much, yet rewarded in like measure.*

*And now, I travel a different road, a road with a purpose
and destination known only to God. but still there is
faith that this road, this journey, seen now only faintly
as through a mist, will one day take form and become
reality.*

*Still, often, I travel back in time on the wings of memory,
and in the vistas of the mind relive those glory days
and feel the gratitude that comes with hindsight.*

I remember! I surely do! Thank you Lord!

Darrell J. Ahrens

FOREWORD

I am writing this for my grandchildren and for their children. My son and daughter have urged me on a number of occasions to provide a written account of some of my most memorable experiences as a fighter pilot as part of our family history for their children and grandchildren. I have not done so up to now out of concern that doing so might be construed as an ego trip. And then I recalled an event that occurred some years ago that changed my mind. It was while I was en route to an assignment in Spain. I stopped off in Nebraska for a few days to visit my mother. While there, we were invited to a small family gathering at the farm of my cousin. While waiting for dinner, I noticed a large bound book on the stand next to where I was sitting. I started skimming through it. It was a history of Platte County, the county in Nebraska where I was raised.

The book consisted mainly of short biographies of the men and women who had been instrumental in settling the county and shaping its government, economy, culture, and religious life. I skimmed through quickly until I came to the biography of a man named John Henry Wurdeman. Whereas the other biographies consisted of a few short paragraphs, two to three pages were devoted to this gentleman. As I read on, I became fascinated with the account of this man's life.

John Henry was raised in Illinois and was only sixteen or seventeen years old when the Civil War broke out. He joined an Illinois regiment and, as I recall, fought in major battles, including Antietam. He was wounded twice, once in the face and, as I remember, once in the leg, and bore the scars for the remainder of his life. After the war, he moved to Nebraska, settled in what is now

Platte County, and became one of the major founding fathers of an agricultural community that expanded in size and grew in importance. He was a dominant influence in the political, economic, and religious life of the region. Primarily through his efforts, a Lutheran pastor was called from Germany to Platte County and the first Lutheran Church was established in the area.

As I read on, I became more and more impressed with John Henry's experiences and accomplishments. Finally, I asked my relatives if any of them knew of this man. One of my elderly aunts looked at me with a surprised expression and said, "Why, Darrell, he was your great grandfather on your dad's side. My aunt went on to say that she could remember sitting on John Henry's lap as a little girl, and she could still picture the scars on his face from the wound. I asked why I had never been told about this man who was my great grandfather. None of my relatives had an answer, and I suspect that they were a little confused as to why I thought it so important to know about him.

I asked where he was buried and learned that his grave was in a little country church cemetery not far from where we were. The next Sunday, after church, I drove to that church cemetery with my two elderly aunts. As I stood there before John Henry's grave, I thought how much I would have liked to have known him, to have had the opportunity to listen to him tell about his exploits and experiences. I wished that he had left some written memoirs for me to read and enjoy and come to know him through them.

The experience made me see more clearly the importance of family history. We seem to have lost sight of that fact in today's fast-paced, mobile society, with its record number of broken families and relationships. The continuity, stability, sense of identity and belonging associated with strong family values and ties and a family history are vital, I believe, to a healthy individual and healthy society. Through such knowledge, both the good and the not-so-good, we come to know more about ourselves.

Remembering how I wished that my great grandfather had left some written account for later generations, I decided then that one day I would contribute to my family history by giving a written account of some of my more memorable experiences. I do not do this out of inflated self-pride or ego, since I know many of my pilot peers who did more than I, and who survived more harrowing experiences, both in combat and non-combat flying. I do this simply to leave a family record, and also out of gratitude that a gracious God granted me my boyhood dream and allowed me to see, do, and experience many things that relatively few get to see, do, and experience.

And who knows? Perhaps one day in the distant future, a young man or woman will read this and say to himself or herself, "I wish I could have known my great grandfather Darrell."

INTRODUCTION

My earliest recollections go back to when I was five or six years old. Although these are few and somewhat sketchy, one clear memory I have is that even then, I wanted to fly, and specifically, I wanted to be a fighter pilot.

This was during the latter years of World War II, and I still remember the patriotic movies, radio programs, and articles and pictures in magazines such as *Life* and *Saturday Evening Post* that extolled the courage and sacrifice of our military personnel. My heroes were all military figures, especially the fighter pilots who captivated and thrilled my imagination.

I had models of aircraft I had built scattered throughout our old house. Periodically, Mom would put her foot down and make me get rid of some of them. I would take them to the roof of our chicken coop, stick matches in the wings and fuselage, set them on fire and sail them off the roof, all the while picturing air battles in my child's imagination. I also leaped from the roof of that chicken coop on one occasion, testing a parachute a friend and I had made out of a bed sheet. The bed sheet did not blossom in the wind like a parachute as I thought it would, and I hit the ground very hard. It felt like I had broken both my legs, which fortunately was not the case. My friend had talked me into being the first, and as it turned out, the only one to try it out. That should be ample testimony as to which one of us was smartest.

As the years passed, this desire to fly grew stronger and stronger. I knew somehow that I had to do that, and felt sure that I would do that, but I had no idea how to go about pursuing that goal. I remember when I was somewhere around thirteen years old, I wrote a letter to the Chief of Staff of the Air Force, asking how I could become a fighter pilot. Lo and behold, I got an answer, from some junior staff officer in the Pentagon I'm sure, encouraging me in my goal and telling me to check with the Air Force when I got old enough for military service.

During my high school years, I think I read every book in the school library on World War II, especially the books on the air wars over Europe and the Pacific. This further fueled my desire to fly. However, during these years, another dominant influence on my life was my Christian faith. My zeal and my readiness to engage in heated debate (in other words, argument) in defense of the central doctrines of the faith caused my poor parents to think I was about to go radical on them.

In the small midwestern town where I grew up, high school counselors did not know much about the options available to a young person who wanted to be a fighter pilot, such as the Academies, ROTC, OTS, etc. High school graduation came, and I had no clear idea of what to do to reach my goal. However, I knew that college was a first step, so on the advice of the Christian school principal at our church, I entered a Christian teacher's college.

I was doing fine in college, but after a year and a half, I got bored. A friend and I decided to join the Marines, which we were sure would offer some excitement and adventure. My friend backed out at the last minute and joined the Navy while I enlisted in the Marines. I had two personal reasons for choosing the Marines. One was that I had heard the Marines needed pilots, and therefore the chance of being selected for pilot training in the Marines was greater than in the Navy or Air Force. The other reason was that Marine Corps boot camp was recognized as much tougher than the boot camp of any other service. As I discovered later, "brutal" would have been a more apt word than "tough" to describe Marine basic training at the time.

As a teenager, I'd acquired the nickname "Sparrow" because of my small, skinny body (I weighed no more than 120 lb. when I enlisted a few months before my nineteenth birthday). Because I'd endured numerous jibes and insults over my small stature, I wanted to prove to both family and friends that I had what it takes to be a Marine. One particular experience during my freshman year in high school especially hurt and embarrassed me at the time. My high school dream was to be a sports jock, but my spindly stature prevented this. My homeroom class included many of the football jocks, and the class instructor was the football coach. He was a big, burly man whom the jocks adored. One morning that football coach called me to the front of the class. He then lifted me up, cradled me in his arms like a baby, and while rocking me back and forth, sang "Rock-a-bye baby." The football jocks and other students in the room broke out in loud, boisterous laughter. I wanted to die on the spot.

Thinking back on it, despite the embarrassment and hurt, it was one of the best things that happened to me. It instilled in me an intense desire to prove that "Sparrow" could accomplish things greater than my hecklers could imagine, greater than being a high school sports jock. My later decision to join the Marines partially stemmed from this desire.

In boot camp, I gained 20 lb. of muscle. I was selected as Right Guide, or recruit leader, of the platoon, and was one of two recruits promoted to PFC upon graduation. I was also promoted to corporal before my two-year active duty tour was finished. My tour in the Marines would in itself comprise a small book of memories and confessions; however, suffice it to say that one of the accomplishments I take a lot of pride in is the fact that I was a United States Marine.

After boot camp, I was assigned to a 155mm. artillery battalion as a radio operator. When my enlistment was up, I was asked to reenlist by the Gunny Sergeant. He noticed that I had applied for pilot training and had taken and passed the associated written aptitude tests, and he told me that if I reenlisted they would consider getting me orders to Pensacola for cadet pilot training. I told them that if they first gave me orders to Pensacola, I would then reenlist. He said, "No! You have to reenlist first." And with that, I took my honorable discharge and became a civilian again.

I spent a year working on a traveling steel construction crew, after which I returned to college and eventually was hired as a production planner with General Dynamics Corp., which was under contract with the Department of Defense to install Atlas Intercontinental Ballistic Missile sites in Nebraska, Kansas, and Oklahoma. Throughout those years, however, I never lost my intense desire to fly and become a fighter pilot.

While with General Dynamics in Altus, Oklahoma, I realized that if I was going to pursue that goal, I had better get with it since I was 25 years old and the maximum age for entering pilot training was 26½ years. This time I tried the Air Force. I went to see the recruiter, told him of my goal, and asked what I had to do to be accepted for pilot training. He informed me that the Air Force didn't need pilots, that missiles were the weapon of the future, and that fighter pilots were becoming obsolete. Instead, he tried to interest me in other Air Force career fields. This was in 1962, and as I write this today, over fifty years later, fighter pilots are still at the point of the spear and the cream of the crop. I informed the recruiter that the only thing I was interested in was flying, and specifically flying in the cockpit of a jet fighter.

With that, the realization dawned on me that my boyhood dream would probably not be realized. But then, a series of events occurred that many would consider as pure coincidences, but which I attribute to the Good Lord's control of circumstances, since I don't believe in coincidences or luck. First, it so happened that one day I shared my dream and my disappointment with a fellow co-worker and friend at General Dynamics. He just happened to have a brother who flew with the Washington Air National Guard. I had never heard of the Air National Guard (ANG). He told me that the Air

Guard units normally received a number of slots for each Air Force pilot training class. Those selected for these slots go on active duty with the Air Force for pilot training and advanced training and then return to their Air Guard units for the final upgrade to mission ready status. They then have a commitment for a certain number of years to the Air Guard and Air Force. He suggested that I call the Air Guard unit in my home state (Nebraska) and ask if they had any pilot training slots available.

I did this, and it just so happened that the unit had three pilot training slots available for classes beginning in January 1963. It also was the case that the unit was flying fighters. I informed the commander of my background, education, and lifelong desire to be a fighter pilot. At his request, I flew to Lincoln, Nebraska, to meet with unit personnel, fill out the application paperwork, and complete other administrative tasks. The unit then made arrangements for me to receive a flight physical at Altus Air Force Base where I was working with General Dynamics, as well as take the day-long written tests for officer qualification and pilot aptitude qualification at Sheppard Air Force Base, Wichita Falls, Texas. This I did and passed both the physical and the written tests. I was sure I had flunked but learned later I had done well.

I then had to return to the unit in Nebraska to meet a formal board that would make the final decision whether or not to offer me a pilot training slot. Thankfully, their decision was yes. After I was informed of my acceptance, I asked if I had to go through Air Force basic training before being commissioned as an officer. The board president laughed and said that anyone who had been through Marine boot camp had no need of any further basic training. I would receive a direct commission as a 2nd Lieutenant.

Obviously, all this took time and money, with the cost of those airline tickets back and forth coming out of my pocket, not to mention the cost of some extensive dental work required before I took the flight physical. I figure it cost me between $600 and $700 to get into pilot training, which in 1962 was a considerable sum of money. But it so happened that I had the money because of my job at General Dynamics.

As far as time was concerned, I had to take a lot of time off work to accomplish all this. But it just so happened that I had a very understanding boss named Bill Utley. When I apologized to him one day for the time I was taking off from work, he told me, "Darrell, don't worry about it. If you have a chance to be accepted for Air Force pilot training, by all means go for it. Take all the time you need, and I will support you all the way." I have always been grateful to Mr. Utley for his understanding and support.

I have recounted all this to make this point. Often, when faced with what appears to be insurmountable obstacles, the human tendency is to give up. Now I'm not saying that there is nothing a person cannot do. That's unrealistic. I do believe, however, that the steps of a person are ordered by the Lord, and if we seek His counsel, He will make us know if our goal does or does not conform to His will. And if it does, there is no obstacle, no matter how formidable or insurmountable it may seem, that will prevent our accomplishing it in His timing if we just don't give up. It is also good to remember that even when we feel assured that our goals conform to His will, He will often allow those seemingly insurmountable obstacles to confront us to test our faith and trust since through such testing, we build character, perseverance, and endurance.

A good rule is to follow the advice of Sir Winston Churchill, who, in the course of his amazing life and career, faced many seemingly insurmountable obstacles. I believe it was when he was addressing a graduating class at a university in the U.S. that Churchill told the students, "Never give in, never give in, never, never, never—in nothing, great or small, large or petty—never give in except to convictions of honor and good sense."

Finally, speaking of the Lord's timing, within a short time after I received orders in August 1962 to report to Reese Air Force Base,

Texas, on January 13, 1963, as a member of pilot training class 64-E, I received notification from General Dynamics that since the Atlas missile program was coming to an end, I and many others would be laid off effective the end of September 1962. And so, it turned out, I had a three-month vacation before entering pilot training and beginning the fulfillment of that boyhood dream.

NOTE TO READER

During a twenty-four-year career as a fighter pilot, one acquires a large store of memories to reflect on and confessions to be made. I have selected only those that stand out in my mind and are especially meaningful to me to be included in this book.   The non-combat flying memories and confessions are presented in chronological order. The combat flying memories and confessions are randomly inserted throughout this chronology in order to provide a mix of the two.

CHAPTER 1

FEAR (F-105)

It was the first and only time I got sick in an aircraft. The cause was not spatial disorientation, vertigo, or any other condition common to flight. The cause was stark fear.

My wingman and I were called to provide fire suppression for a rescue operation to recover the pilot and weapons system officer of an F-4 Phantom shot down in an area bordering North Vietnam and Laos. The area was known as a particularly hot area with lots of enemy anti-aircraft activity, and where a substantial number of aircraft had previously been shot down. We had already expended our bombs on another target, but we both had full loads of 20mm. cannon ammunition in our F-105 fighters. We immediately took up a heading to the area and pushed the power up. The voice of that rescue commander calling for support left no doubt that that F-4 crew was in a very bad situation.

Upon arrival, we were advised of the downed crew's location and told that there were numerous enemy gun sites in the vicinity and lots of enemy activity to face before the Americans could be rescued. The gun sites had to be dealt with before a rescue helicopter could dare attempt flying to the downed crew's position. Bombs would have been the preferred ordnance, but we had no bombs, only cannon shells. Other aircraft with bombs were on the way, but it was critical to attack those enemy positions immediately to slow or halt their progress toward the downed F-4 crew. So we were asked to strafe—that is, to rake those enemy positions with cannon fire.

The Vulcan cannon in the F-105 was a six-barrel gatling gun, hydraulically driven with a high rate of fire of six thousand rounds a minute, 100 rounds a second, and a low rate of fire of four thousand rounds a minute. However, even with such awesome fire power, it was extremely dangerous to strafe anti-aircraft sites since those guns had a longer range than our cannon. The odds heavily favored those gunners getting hits on your aircraft before you got into range to fire at them. Thus, the standard operating procedure was no strafing anti-aircraft sites.

On the other hand, standard operating procedures usually went out the window during a rescue operation. Pilots did not hesitate to take risks beyond the norm, or as the saying goes, "to hang their asses out" to help rescue a brother flyer. The reason was simple. That might be you on the ground tomorrow, hoping and praying to be rescued, and that your brother flyers would hang their asses out for you.

I would roll in on the target first, with my wingman rolling in moments after from a different direction to divide those gunners' attention. I adjusted the gunsight, checked armament switches set, selected a high rate of fire to get the maximum number of shells on target, and flipped the master arm switch to "arm," giving me a hot trigger switch on the control stick. I made a tight 5 to 6 G roll-in, and immediately after I was established in my dive to the target, I saw red-hot anti-aircraft tracer shells flying past my canopy. It was normal procedure for both the enemy and us to coat every fourth or fifth shell of ammunition with a flammable substance so that when it was fired, it would leave a red trail marking its path. In that way, both the enemy and we could follow our shells' trajectory and correct as required. For every tracer you see, you can be sure there are three or four other shells along with it that you don't see.

I had seen tracers flying past before. It's exciting and gets the adrenalin pumping, but like the saying goes, "it's the one you don't see that gets you." That's the one called the "golden BB." I fired a long burst of cannon shells into the enemy's position and immediately started a hard 6 to 7 G pullout and a hard turn to the left to avoid flak coming up from behind me. It was then that I saw a sight awesome to behold, and one that made an indelible impression on me that I carry in my mind's eye to this day.

As I pulled my F-105 into the violent turn and was looking left, I saw a veritable wall of tracer shells extending from behind my aircraft to around the side and to the front flying past me. The visual impression was that of being in a rainstorm with sheets of rain coming down. Only this was a rainstorm of flak coming up at me. Instantly, the seeming impossibility of flying through such a hailstorm of flak without taking multiple hits crossed my mind, and I violently reversed my turn to the right, fully expecting momentarily to feel the thump, thump of shells hitting my aircraft, and that I would either be dead or floating down in my parachute to join that F-4 crew. I rolled out of the high G turn, lit the afterburner, and clawed for altitude to get beyond the range of those guns. Then I realized that somehow, by the grace of God I'm sure, both my wingman and I came through that storm of flak without taking a hit.

My wingman and I both had ammunition left, and the enemy was still moving toward that F-4 crew. Other aircraft with bombs had not yet arrived, so the rescue commander asked us to make another strafing pass to hold off the enemy until those aircraft arrived to provide cover and fire suppression.

Now that was the last thing I wanted to do in view of what we had flown through during the previous attack. Nevertheless, we had ammunition remaining, we had an important target, and there was an F-4 crew in desperate straits and in need of additional fire support to keep the enemy from reaching their position. Given all that, the decision was a no-brainer. We agreed and maneuvered to take up position for another attack.

Then it happened! Realizing that the odds of flying through a similar hailstorm of tracers a second time without taking numerous hits were slim indeed, I was gripped by a wave of nausea and my mouth filled with the bile that comes just before vomiting. I was in position to roll-in on the target, so there wasn't time to unhook my oxygen mask, spit out the bile on the cockpit floor, and hook the mask back up. There was only one thing to do. I swallowed it, fought off the nausea and urge to vomit, and concentrated on the attack.

My wingman and I expended all our ammunition on that attack, and much to our surprise, we didn't see any tracers coming at us. The reason, we figured, was that those gunners had fired everything they had at us on the first pass and had not had time to reload. Or perhaps those gunners weren't expecting a second strafing pass, thinking no pilot would be dumb enough to risk flying a second time through the solid curtain of tracers we had flown through the first time.

After we landed and were riding back to the squadron in the flight line van, my wingman and I just looked at one another, he undoubtedly, like me, wondering how we had come through that unscathed. Then, in a soft, hushed and reverent voice, he said, "Jesus!" His tone was one of awe, as if acknowledging it was due to the intervention of the Lord that we had not been shot down.

When the intelligence debriefer asked for an estimate of how many anti-aircraft rounds had been fired at us, we laughed. Given that wall of tracers, and the fact that for every tracer shell there were three or four more shells, the number could have been close to a thousand. Intelligence had confirmed that the Russians had provided the North Vietnamese the ZSU-23 low altitude air defense system, consisting of two 23mm. cannons on a twin-wheeled carriage. Maximum rate of fire was 1,000 rounds per minute.

Normally a four-gun battery opened fire at a range of about 1,000 meters, or 3,000 feet, which is right at the range we opened fire. Thus, the hailstorm of flak we encountered would correspond with the capability of the ZSU-23 system.

It took a while for the adrenalin to subside. Sir Winston Churchill was right when he said, "There is nothing so exhilarating as to be shot at, without result." I don't remember if that F-4 crew was rescued or not.

Capt. Darrell J. Ahrens
Combat Fighter Pilot / F-105 Thunderchief
34th Tactical Fighter Squadron
388th Tactical Fighter Wing
Vietnam War

CHAPTER 2
FIRST FLIGHT
(T-37)

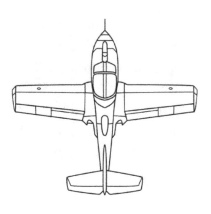

My pilot training class consisted of individuals of just about every personality profile, as well as size and physical description, you could name. As I recall, the height limit for pilot candidates was slightly taller than six feet, and the weight limit a little over 200 pounds due to the relatively small size of the cockpit and the capability of the ejection seats.

A few of my classmates came close to those limits. The others ranged from tall and slender to short and round. As for myself, I was 5 feet 9 inches tall and weighed in at around 150 pounds. All of us found the cockpit quite comfortable in spite of being somewhat small and cramped.

Their personalities, however, covered the gamut. There were those from New York and other cities of the east with their distinct accents and mannerisms who perhaps thought themselves a little wiser in the ways of the world than the rest of us. There were those from the Midwest, unpretentious in speech and manner, a few of whom one could picture on the farm plowing the north forty. There were those from the South with their southern drawl and systematic, methodical habits of expression and action. There were a few Texans who thought Texas was the center of the universe. And there were those from the West Coast, informal and free-spirited who missed the beach and found west Texas to be another planet.

We had our Hawaiian who showed us a picture of himself prior to his entry into the military. He had long, scraggly hair, a drooping mustache, something of a beard, and a deep tan. He admitted that in civilian life he had been a surf bum, albeit an educated one. We had three German Air Force classmates who exhibited just a touch of that famous Prussian arrogance, but not in an offensive way. One of them considered himself quite the ladies' man. They were a welcome addition to the class and quickly picked up American slang expressions.

And then we had a tall, blonde classmate of Scandinavian descent, Norwegian I believe, who looked as if he had been a model for some muscle magazine and who considered himself God's gift to women, especially to the co-eds at Texas Tech University that was located in Lubbock, Texas.

Only two or three met the typical Hollywood stereotype of the fighter pilot—blonde, blue-eyed, and slight of build. I was one of them, except in my case the blonde hair was rapidly disappearing.

The class quickly bonded together despite these differences in personality, and this bond grew stronger with the constant daily stress and pressure to perform. Then too, watching fellow classmates wash out of the program as we progressed drew those of us remaining even closer.

At last the day came when we pilot trainees were to get our first flight in the T-37 jet trainer. We'd spent our first month in pilot training mostly in the classroom, with courses in aviation physiology and T-37 engineering and aerodynamics, as well as in the simulator operating the various aircraft systems and becoming intimately familiar with both normal and emergency operating procedures. We now began a schedule where half the day was devoted to classroom academics and the other half to flying and other squadron activities.

The T-37 was a small two-engine jet trainer with a top speed of around 400 mph. Slower than many of the propeller-driven fighter aircraft of World War II, it was, as many called it, a baby jet. Yet, to us novice military pilot trainees, it was as formidable as a front-line war machine. And on this day, we were to get our first flight in the jet, commonly referred to as our dollar ride.

We were all a bit anxious and nervous and determined to make the best possible impression on our instructor pilot. One of the ways to do that, we were told, was to get to the aircraft ahead of the instructor, have the aircraft forms checked, and be ready to start the preflight when he arrived. This not only demonstrated a take-charge attitude, but also showed aggressiveness, motivation, and eagerness to fly, qualities absolutely essential for military pilots, which the instructors not only wanted in their student charges, but insisted they demonstrate. Without these qualities, the student would invariably wash out of the pilot training program, considered one of the most—if not the most—demanding, high-pressure training programs in the military.

I was determined to make such a favorable first impression on my instructor, Lt. Richard Norton, call sign "Hangover," so that after the flight, he would look to heaven and thank the Lord for the blessing of having 2nd Lieutenant Ahrens assigned to him as one of his students. After the flight briefing, I hurried to the life support section to get my parachute , helmet, and oxygen mask. I gave them a quick inspection and then hurried to the flight line to catch one of the vans that would take me to the parking spot of our assigned aircraft. Knowing that I was well ahead of my instructor, I looked forward to impressing him on his arrival at the aircraft with a smart salute and crisp report, "Aircraft forms are checked, sir, and I'm ready to conduct the preflight."

As I indulged in this self-congratulation for my preparation and foresight, I realized that the flight line van was heading in the opposite direction from where our aircraft was parked. In my zeal, I had hopped on the first van that had come by instead of waiting for one going in the right direction. *Oh well, no sweat*, I thought. The van would reach the end of the flight line, turn around, and head for the opposite end where our aircraft was parked. I had plenty of time and could still reach the aircraft well ahead of my instructor.

Then, as the van reached the wrong end of the flight line, the driver parked and shut off the engine. "What are you doing"? I yelled. "My jet is parked at the other end." "Sorry," the driver said. "My shift is ended. The relief driver will be here in a little while." I pleaded with him to take me to the other end of the flight line, that I didn't have time to wait for another driver. My pleas had no effect on him. He got out of the van and walked away. As I waited, and waited, for the relief driver who wasn't in sight, I was acutely aware of time slipping away, and with it, my plan to make that good impression on my instructor.

Finally, with no relief driver in sight and my plan rapidly going down the toilet, I jumped from the van, and with that heavy parachute banging against my back and butt, I began running the mile or so to the opposite end of the flight line where our jet was parked. As I approached the jet, I saw my instructor looking around, undoubtedly wondering what happened to his errant student. When I arrived, gasping for breath and feeling like I was about to have a stroke, he said, "Hurry up and get strapped in Ahrens. I've checked the aircraft forms and completed the preflight; we're running late.

The flight went well, and the instructor seemed pleased with my performance. During the debriefing, he asked, "Ahrens, what took you so long getting to the jet?" There was no way I was going to tell him I took a flight line van going in the wrong direction from where the jet was parked. I gave him the weak excuse that I took some time checking the status of my parachute, helmet, and oxygen mask. His response was, "A thorough check of your life-support equipment is good, Ahrens, but remember, you're only using that equipment, not buying it. From now on, be at the aircraft on time." My reply was a loud and clear "Yes, sir!" Mine was only one of a number of mishaps by the students on that day of our first flight.

I never told my instructor or classmates about that incident. I knew I would never live it down if they knew. I remembered the story about an aviator named Corrigan in the early days of flying who took off from the east coast for a destination in the western U.S. and ended up in Ireland. From then on, he was known as "Wrong-way Corrigan." I could just imagine the nickname my classmates, not to mention the instructors, would tag on me—"Wrong-way Ahrens." I wasn't about to chance that.

CHAPTER 3
FIRST SOLO
(T-37)

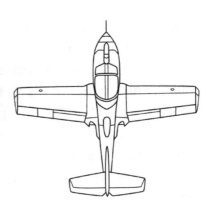

The first milestone in our flying training that we all were anxiously awaiting was upon us—first solo in the T-37. We looked forward to it with anticipation mixed with dread. Few, if any of us, thought we were ready to solo, but it didn't matter what the students thought. The instructors knew if we were ready or not.

Getting the jet in the air wasn't the source of our concern; it was getting it and ourselves back on the ground in one piece that had us worried. The thought of that empty seat next to us, normally occupied by the instructor, was not comforting. The instructor was our safety net. No matter what dire circumstances occurred in flight, whether caused by an aircraft system malfunction or the student doing something stupid, we knew that the instructor would handle it in a professional manner and save the day.

Later in my flying career, when I was an instructor in the F-4 Phantom jet fighter, I would recall that attitude of total trust in the instructor we pilot trainees had. I appreciated the irony because my students had the same attitude toward me—that whatever happened in that war machine, I could handle it. And I wasn't about to dissuade them of that attitude, even though I knew better.

We student pilots knew we were about to face the moment of truth when, after landing and pulling into the parking slot, the instructor would tell us to shut down the engine on his side so he could exit the aircraft but to leave the engine on the student's side running. When my time came, I distinctly remember wanting to tell the instructor, "Sir, if it's all the same with you, I would rather not do this today." But saying that would have shown a lack of confidence and aggressiveness, not to mention the embarrassment to both myself and the instructor. And so, after the instructor exited the aircraft, I restarted the right engine and taxied out to the runway, convinced that I might be living my last day in this life.

After being cleared onto the runway, I shoved the throttles to full power, holding the brakes with shaky legs. I checked all the instruments and gauges, the fuel, oil, hydraulics, flaps, etc., closer than I had ever checked them before, keenly sensitive to the slightest variation in the readings, even hoping for an erratic reading, for that would have been a valid reason to abort and postpone the moment of truth to another day. But alas, everything was as it should be.

With the "cleared for take-off" call from the tower controller, I had two choices—release the brakes and start the take-off roll, or pull the power back, taxi off the runway, and proceed to the parking spot. Reduced to its simplest terms, the choice was either going for it or wimping out. Since going for it was the only macho choice, I started the take-off roll.

Once I became airborne, habit and weeks of memorization of procedures took over. The aircraft was responding beautifully to my every control input, and I felt a surge of pride at being master over machine. I proceeded to my assigned operating area and put the aircraft through a variety of acrobatic maneuvers, climbing, diving, aileron rolls, loops, Immelmans, barrel rolls, etc. After a time, with confidence and comfort level growing exponentially, I headed back to base to enter the traffic pattern.

There were specific checkpoints, procedures, and radio calls associated with entering the traffic pattern. Thinking I had accomplished these with perfection—mistakenly as it turned out, I rolled out on a three-mile initial leg in line with the runway and requested clearance for a touch and go landing. Upon receiving clearance and arriving at a point fifteen hundred feet above the end of the runway, I rolled the aircraft into a sharp 180-degree breaking turn and rolled out on the downwind leg of the pattern. Pleased with myself that I had held the proper altitude (or close to it) throughout the turn, I extended landing gear and flaps, checked safe indications, and when abeam a point just past the end of the runway, called "Base, gear check, touch and go!"

After receiving clearance from the tower, I started my base to final turn, confirmed gear and flaps down, checked fuel status and established the proper final approach speed. Upon reaching the end of the runway, I gradually reduced power while bringing the control stick back slowly to establish the proper landing attitude. And, wonder of wonders, the aircraft touched down—quite smoothly, if my memory is correct. In my excitement and surprise at being in one piece, not to mention smug self-satisfaction, my brain took a momentary break and I forgot that I had been cleared for a touch and go. Regaining my wits, I shoved the throttles forward and, in a short time, was airborne again. I flew two or three more patterns with touch and go landings before fuel status made it necessary to request a full-stop landing.

As I recall, my landings received good grades on that first solo flight, although probably not as good as I like to remember. After landing and while taxiing back to the parking spot, to say I was on cloud nine would be an understatement. I felt intensely alive with an adrenalin rush like nothing I had experienced before. Little did I know that my inflated ego was about to undergo a bit of deflation.

My self-pride in what I considered an outstanding performance took something of a beating and humbling during the flight debriefing with my instructor who, with other instructors whose students were soloing, had been in the mobile control unit alongside the runway monitoring our traffic patterns and landings.

Apparently, during my entry into the traffic pattern, my concentration was so fixated on what I was doing that I neglected to scan the area for other traffic. When entering the initial leg of the pattern, I turned in front of a flight of four aircraft already established on initial. The proper procedure was for me to give way to that flight by turning in behind them and adjusting spacing. As it turned out, they had to break out of the pattern and reenter. The instructors in that flight weren't pleased, to put it mildly. However, as we later found out, the instructors were very much aware of when first-time solos were in the air. They not only expected mistakes caused by those solo trainees' excitement and fixation but anticipated them and made a point of being extra cautious at those times. In fact, the instructors often laughed at the dumb mistakes initial solos made, referred to the skies as dangerous when solos were in the air, and took pleasure in deflating our egos.

My second mistake was even more embarrassing. The call sign of our squadron was "Throttle Jock." On my solo flight, my call sign was "Throttle Jock 21." Yet, during the entire flight, whenever I made or answered a radio call, I would identify myself as Throttle Jockey 21. Now Throttle Jock 21 sounds considerably more macho than Throttle Jockey 21, wouldn't you agree? Apparently, the instructors and the other students thought so because I took an unmerciful ribbing over that.

Hanging on the wall in the squadron briefing room was the "boner board," which listed all the student pilots' names, with a long line of small square boxes behind each name. Every time a student made a mistake, the instructor would charge him a certain number of boners—in other words, mark the appropriate number of squares with an "x." In my case that day, the instructor had me place my head against the boner board. He made a mark on each side of my head, and then had me place an "x" in the number of squares equal to the width of my head. The lesson, of course, was to remind me to use all the gray matter when flying.

But I wasn't alone that day acquiring boners. Everyone who soloed contributed generously to the boner board. Each square signified 25 cents or 50 cents, I forget which, and at the end of the six-month T-37 phase of training, and before going on to the T-38 phase, the boners for each student were tallied. The total amount was used for a grand squadron party to celebrate the successful completion of 131 hours of transition, instrument, navigation, formation, and night training in the T-37 aircraft.

No matter how many boners we collected, it couldn't dampen our enthusiasm one bit. After all, it was only money, and what was that compared to the fact that we had soloed the jet. We who soloed that day were taken to the Officer's Club swimming pool and thrown in for the traditional solo dunking.

There would be many times in the future when I would experience a strong feeling of accomplishment in the air, but the satisfaction and feeling of accomplishment that day when I first soloed the jet was something special that I will never forget.

CHAPTER 4

A MEMORABLE SPIN (T-37)

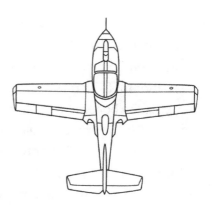

We pilot trainees had reached the point in our T-37 training where we were scheduled for our first check-ride with a Standardization Evaluation check pilot. To pass the check-ride, we had to demonstrate proficiency in all normal operating procedures, in various maneuvers and acrobatics such as chandelles, lazy-eights, aileron rolls, loops, immelmanns, barrel rolls, spin recovery, and finally, in traffic patterns and landings. We students viewed check-rides with considerable trepidation and prepared for them with lots of last-minute cramming, reviewing, and memorizing of normal and emergency operating procedures, aircraft performance specifications, system limitations, etc. The policy in pilot training was that if you failed a check-ride, you would be given a re-check. If you failed that, you would be given an elimination check-ride. If you failed that, you were washed out of pilot training. The policy was the same for written examinations. Fail an exam three times, and you were history.

My check-ride was going well. The check-pilot seemed pleased with my procedural knowledge and my performance of the air maneuvers and acrobatics. He then told me to climb to 20,000 feet, put the aircraft into a spin, and recover. You enter a spin by first stalling the aircraft where the jet no longer has sufficient speed for level flight, and then by pushing the rudder pedal to the floor—left rudder for a spin to the left, right rudder for a spin to the right.

A spin is a violent out-of-control situation with rapid changes in aircraft movement around its three axes of flight—pitch, roll, and yaw—while the aircraft is in a rapid downward spiral. It is very disorienting and confusing due to the severity of the pitch, roll, and yaw oscillations. Spins were prohibited in all Air Force aircraft except the T-37, which was designed to allow spins and recovery to be accomplished safely. Apparently, the Air Force powers that be thought it wise for pilot trainees to experience spins and spin recovery just in case they inadvertently entered a spin in whatever aircraft they would be flying after graduation.

As I recall, the spin recovery procedure in the T-37 consisted of four steps, or control inputs. These had to be performed in the exact sequence given. If performed out of sequence, or if one of the control inputs was not accomplished, the result was an accelerated spin or an inverted spin, making recovery all the more difficult. Now I had performed spin recoveries on previous flights with my instructor, and I knew the procedure thoroughly. My confidence was high—too high as it turned out.

After the spin was established, with the aircraft rapidly going round and round, up and down, the check pilot told me to recover. Wanting to show him just how good I really was, I immediately started to accomplish the steps for recovery instead of taking a moment to review the steps in my mind first to ensure I did them properly and methodically. Well, in my rush, I skipped over one of the steps, and the aircraft reacted just as the flight manual warned. It immediately went into an accelerated spin. A normal procedure had now become an actual serious emergency.

The check pilot immediately said, "I've got the aircraft" and took control. He accomplished the spin recovery steps, but the aircraft didn't respond. Meanwhile, we were losing altitude rapidly. It was then I remembered the statement in the checklist following the spin recovery procedure that said, "If the aircraft is not recovered, or not beginning to recover, by 10,000 feet altitude, EJECT! It may be your last chance for survival." Glancing at the altimeter, I noticed that we were passing 10,000 feet in our downward death spiral, and the realization dawned on me that we might have to eject.

Now you might think that the very real possibility of having to eject from that spinning aircraft would have been the primary concern uppermost in my mind at the time. Obviously, it was a major concern, but not the main one. The main concern going through my mind while we were rapidly spinning toward the ground was that if we lost that airplane due to my stupid mistake, I might wash out of pilot training.

The check pilot neutralized the controls and accomplished the spin recovery steps again. The aircraft still didn't respond, and the rate of spin did not decrease. Nor did the rate of descent. Fortunately, the check-pilot did not call for ejection. Instead, he neutralized the controls and again went through the steps for spin recovery. And lo and behold, the spin rate started to slow down, and then stopped. The aircraft was now in a controllable steep dive, and the instructor brought the nose up briskly to straight and level flight. The altimeter indicated between 6,000 and 7,000 feet, and I have no doubt that if the aircraft had not recovered during that third attempt, we would have been floating down in our parachutes shortly afterward.

During the flight debriefing back in the squadron, the check pilot was cool about it. Apparently, having a student put him in a bad situation was not unusual for him. His comment was, "Well, that was a bit exciting!" He had no choice but to give me a failing grade on the flight. It was the only failing grade I got during the 13 months of pilot training.

Before I could re-fly the check ride, I had to fly with another instructor and demonstrate proficiency in spin recoveries. After I performed a few spins with perfect recoveries, the instructor was well satisfied and said, "I've seen enough, let's return to base." I was scheduled for another check-ride the following day and passed it with flying colors.

Some might criticize that instructor for not strictly adhering to the book and not calling for ejection when we passed 10,000 feet. After all, at the rate we were descending, the altitude for recovery was rapidly diminishing. But I admired him for not doing so—and not because it probably saved my flying career. As I came to know and apply later, just about every limitation on the aircraft's performance data given in the flight manual has a margin of safety built in. The mark of a good pilot is both knowing how far he can push that margin while avoiding catastrophe, and being willing to push it when the occasion demands. That check-pilot had both qualities.

Lesson learned for me—be aggressive and confident, but beware of becoming overconfident.

CHAPTER 5

A WILD RIDE (F-105)

The mission was against a target in North Vietnam where intelligence indicated that equipment, ammunition, and supplies for the communists in South Vietnam and Laos were hidden during daytime for protection against airstrikes and then moved under cover of night. We attacked the target with bombs, and then followed up by strafing the area with 20 mm. cannon.

It was standard operating procedure not to make multiple passes against a target since statistics showed that the chances of being shot down increased dramatically with successive attacks. So, after our strafing pass, we started a climbing turn to exit the area. However, since I had ammunition remaining, I decided to expend it on a final attack against the target. I told my wingman to continue climbing on the egress heading and that I would rejoin with him shortly. I then turned back to the target.

I fired all the cannon shells remaining, made a couple of high "G" turns to avoid ground fire, and started a climbing turn, rolling out on a heading to rejoin my wingman. And then, after a short time during the climb, I experienced something that I had never experienced before and would never experience again in an aircraft as far as its violence and intensity were concerned.

It started out as a tremor, a vibration that I felt in the cockpit. My first thought was that I had taken a hit. Then suddenly, the aircraft began shaking so violently that I lost control of it. It was as if a giant hand had reached down, grabbed hold of my F-105, and was shaking it to pieces. I looked out at the wings and was amazed to see that they were flapping up and down, and the picture of a bird in flight momentarily crossed my mind. I expected the wings to separate from the fuselage because of the tremendous stress they were surely receiving.

The shaking was so intense and violent that the entire cockpit was a blur, and I was unable to focus on anything. The instrument panel was bouncing and shaking so violently that I was sure it would shake itself off its mounts. Instinctively, I reached out to keep it from falling in my lap. I was terrified and felt totally helpless, and as I recall, I cried out, "Jesus, save me!"

I reached down for the ejection handles, fearing that the aircraft would either immediately explode due to broken fuel lines or disintegrate from the violence of the shaking. But then I hesitated, realizing that I had crossed the border of North Vietnam and was over Laos. Many pilots had been shot down over Laos, something the American people didn't know. That's because our political leaders didn't want them to know that, in addition to Vietnam, a nasty and brutal war was being fought in Laos against the Pathet Lao, the Laotian communists allied with North Vietnam and the Viet Cong.

Very few of the pilots shot down over Laos survived if they weren't rescued within a short time. The intelligence information was that the Pathet Lao normally didn't take prisoners and brutally tortured American pilots to death. The standard operating procedure was not to eject over Laos, if at all possible. If one was hit and had to eject, whether over North Vietnam, South Vietnam, or Laos, the order of priority was as follows: First, if at all possible, and if the aircraft was still controllable, get out over the Gulf and eject. The

Navy would pick you up. Second, if that was not possible, eject over South Vietnam. Hopefully, American forces would get to you before the Viet Cong did. Third, if neither of the above two options was available, eject over North Vietnam. You would be taken prisoner and probably tortured, but the North Vietnamese would not kill you since they used American prisoners for propaganda and political leverage against the United States. Fourth, if no other option was available, eject over Laos.

The first three options were not available to me, given the fact that the aircraft was shaking and gyrating violently and was uncontrollable. However, since the aircraft was still in one piece (a fact that I could only marvel at because of the violence and intensity of the shaking), and since I had no desire to take my chances with the Pathet Lao, I released the ejection handles and decided to stay with the airplane and attempt to get out of Laos.

I attempted to jettison the fuel tanks under the wings to reduce weight, even though the reduction in weight would be minimal with the tanks empty. Even so, getting rid of them would reduce drag and help me gain altitude. On the right console of the cockpit, there were three jettison buttons—one each for the outboard wing stations, the inboard wing stations that carried the fuel tanks, and the centerline fuselage station that carried the Multiple Ejector Rack (MER), which had carried the bombs and was now empty.

The problem, however, was that the aircraft was shaking so violently everything was a blur and indistinct, making it impossible to focus on any particular instrument, control button, or switch. I couldn't align my finger with the proper jettison button or even distinguish between it and the others. I made a wild stab at it and ended up jettisoning the empty bomb rack instead of the fuel tanks.

If I could only gain altitude, and if the airplane held together, and if the engine didn't quit, perhaps I could get across the Laotian border and over Thailand where I could eject safely. But the extreme violence of the shaking and vibration had caused a serious reduction of engine thrust. To get the thrust needed to gain the altitude required, I would have to light the engine afterburner. However, that would spray a huge amount of fuel into the exhaust section where it would become ignited. If the decrease in thrust I was experiencing was due to leaking fuel lines caused by the violent shaking, and if raw fuel was pooled in the engine bay, lighting the afterburner would probably result in both my F-105 and myself becoming a huge fireball.

My only options were to eject or to take the chance of lighting the afterburner, so I said a quick "Lord, help me!" and put the throttle in afterburner. And with great relief, I felt the kick in the pants when the afterburner lit. The airplane didn't blow up or disintegrate, and I got the thrust needed to climb.

Then, almost imperceptibly, I sensed that the violent shaking had eased slightly. After a few moments, suddenly, unexpectedly, it stopped altogether, and I was back in control of the aircraft.

After I landed, the aircraft was put in a hangar, and maintenance gave it a thorough inspection. They found popped rivets, cracked spars, and other damage. I don't know what caused that perfectly performing F-105 to suddenly start trying to shake itself to pieces. Maybe a missile or anti-aircraft shells I didn't see exploded in close proximity and affected the stability augmentation feature of the flight control system, or perhaps it was simply an aircraft malfunction.

I read of a Navy pilot's experience of having a surface-to-air missile (SAM) explode near him, and his description of his aircraft's shaking violently and uncontrollably and his being unable to focus on anything matched exactly what I had experienced.

At any rate, the result was a totally extreme, violent, and uncontrollable wild ride, the likes of which I had no desire to ever experience again.

The M-61 Vulcan 20mm. Gatling gun cannon was an awesome weapon with two rates of fire - high rate of 6,000 shells a minute, 100 a second; and low rate of 4,000 shells a minute.

CHAPTER 6

THE WHITE ROCKET (T-38)

We pilot trainees had finished the T-37 phase of training, accumulating 131 hours of transition, instrument, navigation, and formation and night flying, and capping it off with a squadron party paid for with the "boner" debt each trainee had accumulated during the six months. The class—that is, those of us who hadn't washed out up to this point—moved to the T-38 phase for advanced training.

The T-38 was a pure joy to fly. It was the Air Force's brand new supersonic advanced trainer, and our class at Reese Air Force Base was the second class to fly the T-38. In fact, the base was still receiving its new T-38s from the factory. I recall going to my assigned jet one day and, while checking the forms, discovered that the jet had a total of five flying hours. It had been delivered from the factory a couple of days before. Most classes ahead of us in training were still flying the subsonic T-33, and we lost no opportunity to remind those pilot trainees that we were flying the new T-38. Needless to say, this did not endear us to them.

The T-38 was capable of supersonic (faster than the speed of sound) speed in level flight, something that many of the day's older fighters were not capable of. It was also very light on the controls with instantaneous response to the slightest control input. The common joke was that all you had to do was think about maneuvering and the jet would respond. It had a rate of roll and a climb rate that was awesome to experience. And to top it all off, it was a beautifully designed airplane, esthetically pleasing to the eye with its aerodynamic, streamlined shape.

At the time, the aircraft was painted all white, with orange identification flashes on the nose, wing-tips, and top of the vertical stabilizer. It exuded speed and maneuverability even when parked on the ramp, and whereas its official name was "Talon," it quickly acquired the nickname of "White Rocket."

The T-38 was a quantum leap in design and performance for a jet trainer, and it has been upgraded over time. This is attested to by the fact that as I write more than 50 years later, the T-38 remains the primary advanced jet trainer in the United States Air Force and in some allied air forces. Then too, the T-38's performance and flying qualities were so good that a fighter version, the F-5, was produced and remains in service today with the Air Force and Navy and other air forces around the world.

One of our first acts after moving to the T-38s was to be fitted with a "G" suit, which inflated (no pun intended) our egos even more. Since the high performance of the T-38 entailed experiencing considerable more G forces than in the T-37, the G suit, with inflatable rubber bladders in the thighs and waist, was designed to counteract these forces to some extent. High G forces encountered during rapid and violent maneuvering forced the blood to the lower extremities of the body, in the case of positive Gs, and to the body's upper extremities in the case of negative Gs. With high positive Gs, the result of the blood draining from the upper body initially resulted in tunnel vision, followed by loss of vision, loss of situational awareness, and eventually unconsciousness. The G suit was designed to counteract high positive G forces.

With the onset of G forces, the rubber bladders in the G suit would inflate with air bled from the compressor section of the engines, exerting pressure on the lower body to delay or slow down blood flowing from the upper body to the lower body, thereby allowing the pilot to maneuver effectively under high G forces. The higher the G forces, the greater the inflation of the G suit, with a corresponding increase in the pressure exerted on the lower body.

One gets the sensation of G forces when riding a roller coaster and feel themselves pushed down in the seat - positive Gs, or lifted up from the seat - negative Gs, although the sensation is mild at 2 Gs or less. In a jet fighter, however, with the pilot's body weight 160 lbs., a 7 G turn increases his body weight to 1,120 lbs, the force of gravity pushing him into the seat. Under lower G conditions, the pressure exerted on the pilot's body can be quite comfortable. We fighter pilots insisted that experiencing high G forces was good for one's libido, and the more Gs the better. There is, of course, not one shred of medical evidence to substantiate that theory.

If high G forces—7 or 8 Gs—were maintained for more than a few seconds, the pressure exerted on the lower body could become downright uncomfortable, and even painful. And if those G forces were maintained much longer, even the G suit could not fully counteract the forces and keep the pilot aware and conscious. If the pilot felt himself succumbing to the Gs, all he had to do was ease up on the back-stick pressure and reduce the G forces, and the blood flow to the upper extremities—eyes, brain, etc.—would immediately be restored. However, if he failed to do this and lost consciousness, it could take up to 30 to 45 seconds for him to fully regain consciousness and situational awareness. And an aircraft, especially a high-performance jet, can lose a lot of altitude in 30 to 45 seconds.

There have been more than a few occasions where pilots flew into the ground during those 30 to 45 seconds. This situation became extremely critical with the advent of the F-16, with its fly-by-wire control system, 9-G capability, and instantaneous control response.

We T-38 pilot trainees considered receiving our G suits our entrance into the high-performance area of flight, which in fact it was. Before we could strap on the jet, however, we had to complete the initial academic courses in T-38 flight physiology, engineering, and aerodynamics, as well as spend numerous hours in the simulator practicing normal and emergency procedures. Finally, the big day came for our first flight, or dollar-ride. This initial flight was to be a demonstration of the aircraft's performance, and so the instructor occupied the front cockpit and the student the rear cockpit. I vividly remember my impressions during that first flight. We received clearance for take-off, and the instructor advanced the throttles to full military power and released the brakes. The sensation of power was much greater than in the T-37. The instructor then placed the throttles in afterburner, which gave the maximum thrust on both engines. The acceleration was immediate and rapid, pushing me back in the seat. I glanced at the airspeed indicator, which was already approaching 100 knots. At 140 knots, the instructor lifted the nose, and we were airborne. He immediately raised the landing gear and flaps to avoid exceeding their extension limits. He then stood that aircraft on its tail in a maximum performance climb. It was all so fast that it was somewhat disorienting, and I gripped the canopy rails to maintain equilibrium. In approximately 1 minute 30 seconds, we leveled off at either 30,000 feet or 40,000 feet, I forget which. It all happened so fast that, although my body was at that altitude, my mind and situational awareness were still back at the end of the runway.

After leveling off, with the engines still in afterburner, we went supersonic, exceeding the speed of sound at Mach 1.03. He then slowed down to subsonic speed and gave me the controls, and I did some rolls, tight turns, and acrobatics. The rate of roll was so fast that I had to physically restrain my head and helmet from slamming against the canopy. The pressure of the G suit felt good, and the immediate control response and outstanding maneuverability of the jet made it an absolute delight to fly.

After a little more air-work, we returned to base and the traffic pattern for some touch and go landings. Landing the T-38 was far different from landing the T-37. Whereas the final approach and landing in the T-37 was the same as for any straight-wing aircraft, the T-38, with its thin, short swept wings, was designed to handle and perform like the supersonic fighters. This required a power-on, high angle-of-attack final approach. If the pilot started reducing power when approaching the end of the runway, or let the airspeed get below final approach airspeed while maintaining the required high angle-of-attack, a sink rate developed. If not corrected immediately with power, the inevitable result would be a very hard landing or a crash short of the runway. As it turned out, most of my fellow trainees and I found the power on, high angle-of-attack approach and landing easy to become accustomed to.

After we landed, I remember wondering if I had what it takes to master that superb jet with its speed and performance. However, I need not have been concerned. After the required four or five flights with an instructor, I soloed the T-38 with no problems, as did the majority of the class. Well, I did have one problem during my first solo, although it had nothing to do with handling the jet.

On my first solo flight, while enjoying myself immensely in the acrobatic area doing aileron rolls, loops, immelmanns, and barrel rolls, I failed to notice that a solid undercast of cloud cover was forming below me. When my fuel state had reached the point where it was time to return to base and the landing pattern, I discovered that the undercast was solid and continuous with no holes of clear airspace to descend through while maintaining a visual lookout for other aircraft.

To complicate matters, my Tactical Air Navigation instrument (TACAN), which indicates direction and distance to destination— in this case home base—had malfunctioned. The indicator was spinning erratically, proving that you can't count on everything operating perfectly, even with a brand new aircraft. Without the ability to orient me with visual references to landmarks because of the undercast, and with the TACAN inoperative, I had no idea where I was exactly or what heading to take back to base. And if that wasn't enough to cause stress to a novice military aviator, my fuel state was getting to the point where I would be at minimum fuel status before long.

Descending through solid cloud cover without being under FAA or military radar control was prohibited due to the danger of mid-air collision with another aircraft. The smart thing would have been to check my list of radio frequencies, select a radar control facility, and give them a call requesting a radar monitored descent through the undercast and a vector back to base. But then, I never claimed to be smart at this stage of my flying career. Besides, doing so would have been an admission that I had failed to keep a close eye on the weather as aviators are taught to do from day one, and had painted myself into a corner. Pride prevented this.

Finally, my fuel state dictated that I better do something. So, with a quick prayer that there were no aircraft under me, and that there was plenty of clear airspace below that solid undercast, I lowered the nose and descended through the cloud cover, keeping a close eye on the altimeter. It seemed forever, but I finally got through the solid clouds and into clear airspace. Basic pilotage navigation using landmarks helped me locate a fairly large city in the distance. I took note of the railroad, highway, and other landmark features. After some cross-checking between these landmarks and my local area map, I recall identifying the city as Longview, Texas. With that information, I knew the direction and distance to home base.

I promptly took up a heading to base with my tail between my legs. What I had done was not only stupid but dangerous, and all because of pride. I could say that I learned a lesson from that experience to always keep track of my present position and the direction and distance to destination, and to be prepared for problems. However, in truth, it was a lesson I would have to relearn later when flying the F-100 out of Luke Air Force Base, a memory and confession I will relate in the next section. My favorite phase of flying in the T-38 was formation, and especially four-ship in-trail acrobatics, with each succeeding aircraft's nose just slightly behind and below the exhaust nozzles of the preceding aircraft. To stay in position while the flight leader was doing loops, barrel-rolls, and other maneuvers was hard work requiring continuous flight control and throttle adjustments. It was particularly demanding for the No. 4 pilot because he was at the end of the whip, so to speak, and he had to work harder than the others to stay in position with even larger and more precise flight control and throttle adjustments. I got lots of satisfaction flying that position and staying in formation. I heard that Air Training Command later removed four-ship in-trail formation acrobatics from the flying curriculum. Apparently, they lost an aircraft or two. Too bad! Although a bit dangerous (but what military flying isn't), and very demanding, it was a real confidence and skill builder.

As I recall, the wash-out rate for our class was around 33 percent, including a few who had hurt themselves physically during sports activities. Their flying scores were good, but they were no longer physically qualified for flying status. As for the rest of us, graduation day was approaching when we would receive those silver wings. Each of us approached our last flight in the T-38 with mixed feelings, sad to be leaving that beautiful jet, but greatly relieved and excited over the fact that we had made it through that 13 months of constant stress and pressure in both the flying and academic curricula. We graduated from pilot training with a total of 262 flying hours—131 hours in the T-37 and 131 hours in the T-38.

When I climbed down the ladder of that T-38 after my last flight, I ran my hand affectionately over the wings and fuselage. Then I kissed her on the nose and said good-by to the "white rocket."

"Oh, I have slipped the surly bonds of earth..."

CHAPTER 7
THE HUN (F-100)

fter graduation from pilot training, I reported back to my squadron at the Nebraska Air National Guard. The squadron was preparing for a major command shift from Air Defense Command (ADC) to Tactical Air Command (TAC). They were to be assigned the mission role of Tactical Reconnaissance and would be converting from the F-86L interceptors to RF-84F fighter reconnaissance jets. Since it made no sense to check me out in the F-86L, which they would be losing shortly, and since they had not yet started receiving their RF-84Fs, I was in a period of limbo. But not for long!

One day the Squadron Commander called me into his office and informed me that Tactical Air Command had made available to the unit a training slot in the next class to get checked out in the F-100 at Luke Air Force Base, Phoenix, Arizona. The commander said it would be a good opportunity for me to get some TAC experience, and asked if I wanted the slot. After taking less than a microsecond to consider it, I responded with an exuberant, "Yes, Sir!" Truth be known, I would have crawled through a field of sand burrs for the opportunity to fly the F-100. In those days, if you were a "Hun" pilot, you were somebody, the cream of the crop.

The Hun, the F-100 Super Sabre, was the frontline fighter in TAC and the USAF then. With sharply swept-back wings and a J-57 engine that delivered 16,000 lbs. of thrust in afterburner, it was the first Air Force fighter capable of sustained supersonic speeds in level flight. The jet had also acquired the nickname "widowmaker." It had some flying characteristics that could prove disastrous if the pilot became complacent or tried to manhandle the machine. It also had a landing speed that was considerably higher than in other jet fighters.

The F-100 had been rushed into production and to the squadrons before all the flight testing had been completed and all the bugs discovered and corrected. The Air Force was in a hurry to get the aircraft operational in order to counter the new MiG fighters the Russians were producing. I read somewhere that out of a little more than 2,100 F-100s built, over 800 were lost in accidents alone, not counting the combat losses in the Vietnam War. In other words, it was not a very forgiving aircraft. Nevertheless, even with its reputation of being a widowmaker, the fact that the F-100 was the Air Force's frontline fighter, combined with the fact that it was a challenge to master, only whet the appetites of pilots to strap that machine on and go for it.

One feature of the F-100 was that, with its sharply swept-back wings, the final approach had to be a high angle-of-attack (nose high), power-on approach. Now, that wasn't strange to pilots like me who had flown the new T-38 in pilot training, since it was designed to handle like a supersonic fighter with the same handling and landing characteristics. But the majority of pilots at the time had not flown the T-38 in pilot training. Their advanced trainer had been the T-33, a straight-wing jet. In that jet, you could lower the nose in a slight dive to the runway, pull the throttle back, and raise the nose as you approached the end of the runway. The lift generated by that straight-wing allowed you to float to touchdown, usually without adding any power.

To fly such an approach in the F-100 was a passport to the grave. Lift is not only a function of angle-of-attack (the angle between the chord line of the wing and the relative wind passing over the wings), but also airspeed. In the F-100, if you maintained final approach airspeed by diving at the runway with the throttle back, the result was a rapid loss of airspeed and rapid sink rate when you raised the nose to decrease rate of descent for landing. Why? Because the aerodynamic drag on those sharply swept-back wings exceeded the aerodynamic lift produced by those wings.

With the high sink rate and the aircraft low to the ground in the final stage of the approach to landing, the only possibility of recovery was power (thrust), and lots of it. But the J-57 engine, as powerful, rugged, and reliable as it was, took a few seconds to spool-up and deliver full thrust. And in those few seconds, the sink rate could become so great that not even all 16,000 lbs. of thrust that engine delivered was sufficient to stop the descending sink rate. In such a situation, the pilot, to put it in aerodynamic terms, had "fallen behind the power curve."

And, in this case, to use a fighter pilot term, he had "bought the farm," since there was no escape. The pilot could not lower the nose to gain airspeed and recover because he was so low to the ground there wasn't enough altitude for recovery. He didn't have enough thrust, even with afterburner, to stop the sink rate in time. And if he ejected, the excessive sink rate would prevent the ejection seat from getting him high enough for his parachute to fully deploy. The inevitable outcome was death.

During our first class in F-100 academics, the instructor showed us a film entitled *The Sabre Dance* of an F-100 pilot who had gotten behind the power curve during landing approach. The pilot had pulled the nose of the aircraft way high trying to stop the sink rate. He had the engine in afterburner, evidenced by the long sheet of flame coming from the exhaust section. The wings were rocking back and forth excessively, indicating a stall. Finally, the aircraft rolled to the right and impacted the ground nearly inverted in a gigantic fireball. The instructor's comment to us was, "Gentlemen, don't do this!" As if we needed reminding.

Another insidious characteristic of the F-100 was the aerodynamic phenomenon called "adverse yaw." Under high angle-of-attack, low airspeed flight conditions, when the pilot moved the controls to roll and turn in one direction, the aircraft would abruptly roll in the opposite direction. For example, moving the control stick to the right raises the aileron on the right wing, which reduces lift over that wing and lowers the aileron on the left wing, which increases the curvature of the wing's surface, thereby increasing life. The normal result is a roll and turn to the right. Under high angle-of-attack, low airspeed conditions, however, the aerodynamic drag on the wing with the lowered aileron exceeds the increase in lift on that wing, and that excessive drag is great enough to roll the aircraft in the opposite direction to that intended.

Adverse yaw can be very disconcerting to a pilot, especially when engaged in intense maneuverings, such as in a dogfight. The instinctive tendency when encountering it is to increase the aileron input to overcome the roll in the opposite direction. The result of this is an abrupt snap-roll, followed by a spin if recovery is not immediate. And spin recovery in the F-100 is highly doubtful.

The solution to adverse yaw, which was drilled into our heads, is to avoid aileron inputs during high angle-of-attack, low airspeed flight. Neutralize the ailerons and use the rudder to roll and turn the aircraft. The rudder is highly effective. In fact, the F-100 is known as a "rudder aircraft." You use the rudder to maneuver the F-100 much more than in other aircraft.

Another disconcerting feature of the aircraft concerned its engine, the J-57, which had a tendency to compressor stall when the throttle was advanced too rapidly, especially during extreme maneuvering or low airspeed flight. This was due to disruption of the airflow entering the compressor section of the engine. The stall could range from mild to severe, with a loud bang accompanying it. This got the pilot's attention since the compressor section of the engine was located just below and behind the cockpit. I remember experiencing one compressor stall during a dogfight with another F-100 that sounded like an explosion and was so severe that it knocked my feet completely off the rudder pedals.

Another of my memorable experiences during F-100 training occurred during the air-to-air gunnery phase. We fired on a target called the "dart," which was towed 1,500 feet behind another aircraft. It had a metal frame with four thick wooden wings shaped like an "X." We were cleared to make our firing pass on the dart after the tow pilot entered a turn. This was to avoid any of our shells hitting the tow aircraft. The F-100 had four 20mm. cannons, and you could see if you got any hits from the tell-tale puffs when those cannon shells hit the wooden wings, which had a silver lining.

We had three dart missions during training, and to qualify in that phase, you had to get at least one hit on the target. I had had two missions without a hit and was determined to get a hit on my third mission. The normal firing range from the target was 1,200 feet, with 1,000 ft. being the minimum range for firing. I had a good pass going with the gunsight computing the proper lead angle, distance, etc., and I maneuvered to put the "pipper" (aiming dot) on the target. I passed minimum range and closed to within 800 feet to increase my chances of getting a hit.

And hit it I did, while at the same time scaring the crap out of myself. Hits from those four cannons shredded that dart, with numerous large pieces of those wooden wings flying over the nose intake section and the canopy. It happened so fast I didn't have time to instinctively duck. There were so many pieces that it was well-nigh a miracle none of them went down the intake section of the aircraft. The J-57 was a rugged engine that could take damage and continue operating, but I doubt it could have inhaled large pieces of that dart without catastrophic effects. The instructor on that flight had some strong words about complying with minimum range restrictions, but I got my hit and qualified in the air-to-air gunnery phase.

Another memory (and confession), and one that I would just as soon forget, occurred during my first solo flight in the F-100. Does that sound familiar? It will! My initial flights with an instructor had all gone well, with comments that I handled the aircraft well and should have no problems in the program. These initial flights with an instructor had all been in the Luke AFB southern operating areas. On my first solo flight, however, I was scheduled to operate in the northern airspace operating area. I didn't mention to the scheduler or my instructor that I had never been to the assigned area since I didn't want to appear hesitant or unconfident.

Full of pride and excitement over soloing the current top fighter aircraft in the USAF, I released the brakes, lit the afterburner, and exulted in the kick in the pants given by that 16,000 lbs. of thrust accelerating me down the runway. I complied with all departure procedures and proceeded to the northern operating area where I promptly started to put the aircraft through its paces, with rolls, tight turns, and acrobatic maneuvers. I was confident I could handle that supersonic flying machine and had no doubt I would be able to employ it as a weapon of war.

Alone in that fighter jet, I could relate to the words contained in that epic poem "High Flight" written by a young Spitfire pilot during World War II:

"...slipped the surly bonds of earth"

"...danced the skies on laughter-silvered wings,"

"...flung my eager craft through footless halls of air,"

"...put out my hand and touched the face of God."*

My serenity and excitement were rudely interrupted by two things—I had reached "bingo fuel," meaning it was time to return to base, and I suddenly realized I didn't have a clue where I was, except

---

* From the poem, "High Flight" by Royal Canadian Air Force officer John Gillespie Magee Jr. accessed 9/1/20 at
https://www.lakenheath.af.mil/News/Features/Display/Article/1025699/high-flight-poetry-at-30000-feet/

for the certainty I was somewhere far north of the base. It was all too familiar. The memory of that T-38 solo where I had placed myself in a similar situation briefly crossed my mind. And wouldn't you know it? My TACAN navigation instrument was inoperative, just as it had been on that previous occasion, so I didn't have direction and distance information relative to my present position from the base. The only certainty I had, since I was in the northern operating area, was that the base was south of me.

The only difference between the two situations was that there was no cloud cover this time. Visibility, as normal in Arizona, was unlimited. And so, I again used basic pilotage navigation, trying to find familiar landmarks on the ground to orient myself as to where I was. However, the Arizona terrain below me was far different than the terrain over Texas. Searching the ground for landmarks I could locate on my local area map, all I could see was desert, and it all looked the same. Because the airspace was used for jet fighter training, including air-to-air fighting and supersonic flight, it was located over some unpopulated and very desolate territory. There were no major towns, highways, railroads, or other stand-out landmarks, manmade or otherwise, to cue in on.

Now, again, the smart thing to do would have been to make a radio call to Phoenix Air Traffic Control at Sky Harbor Airport and ask for a vector and distance back to Luke AFB. But I'll say again what I said before, "Who says I was smart at this stage?" Besides, this time I didn't have an undercast of cloud cover to use as an excuse. Making that call would have been a clear admission that I was lost, and I wasn't about to do that—yet. So, taking up a southerly heading, I continued to search that desolate desert landscape for some clue as to where I was, all the while watching my fuel state, which was getting lower and lower. The F-100 burnt fuel at a rapid rate, even at lower power settings.

Before long, I started receiving radio calls from the Luke AFB control tower, asking for my position and an estimate of when I would arrive at the field. I gave them an estimate of 15 minutes. Sure enough, 15 minutes later I received another call asking for my position and estimated time of arrival at the field. I again fudged and gave them a totally unrealistic estimate. Finally, my fuel state had gotten to the point where I was getting somewhat panicked. Gulping down my pride, I called the control tower, informed them that my navigation equipment was inoperative and that I was uncertain of my position (in other words, lost).

The tower diverted another airborne F-100 to find me, which that pilot did by having me key my UHF radio switch and hold it down so his direction finding (DF) feature could home in on my radio signal. Also, he called Phoenix Air Traffic Control, which made radar contact with me and gave him a vector and distance to my position. He soon joined up, and we both headed to base with me flying formation on his wing. I landed with 800 lbs. of fuel remaining, enough for perhaps 10 or 15 minutes of flight.

I was extremely embarrassed over the whole incident, and I could have kicked myself (which I did mentally) for letting my pride override common sense and good judgment. I should have learned that lesson the first time in the T-38 and not have had to relearn it in the F-100. But relearn it I did! From then on, throughout my flying career, I was zealous in maintaining awareness of my position while airborne, and I always tried to have a back-up plan in the event of equipment failure. So I guess all's well that ends well.

The rest of my checkout in the F-100 went without a hitch. I had no serious problems in the various phases of training—dive-bombing, skip-bombing, strafing, simulated nuclear weapons deliveries, air-to-air dogfighting, air-to-air gunnery, and air-to-air refueling. We were all concerned about that first air-to-air refueling and the difficulty of inserting that probe into the small conical receptacle of the tanker at nearly 400 mph and while bouncing around in the air mass trying not to hit the refueling boom or the tanker. As I found out later as an instructor, taking a student up on his first air-to-air refueling mission, and especially on his first night air refueling mission, is not something an instructor looks forward to.

Finally, graduation day arrived, and we received our diplomas as fully qualified F-100 fighter pilots. And with that, I bid adieu to Phoenix. But not for long. During the course of that six months, I became engaged to Louise Irmer, a Lutheran minister's daughter, after about a two-month courtship. I left Phoenix in October 1964 and returned in February 1965 to marry the woman I had fallen in love with. After a short honeymoon in Mexico, we headed for Lincoln, Nebraska and back to my assigned squadron in the Nebr. ANG.

In my introduction to this book, I mentioned the unlikely set of circumstances that all happened to just come together to open a door for me to get into pilot training when all other doors were closed. I attributed those circumstances to God's action rather than mere coincidence or luck since I don't believe in coincidence or luck. Well, a similar situation happened while I was in Phoenix regarding how my wife and I met. The reader will have to forgive me if I engage in a bit of nostalgia.

I was getting a bit tired of the bachelor's life and thinking of finding a wife. I happened to mention this to God in a prayer one day and asked Him to steer me to the wife He had in mind for me. Shortly afterward, I started feeling a bit guilty about having put my Christian faith on the back burner, and I decided to go to church. I checked the phone book for a Lutheran church, as I was raised Lutheran, and picked St. Paul's Lutheran Church, which turned out to be the church where my future wife's father was the minister. I took a seat in one of the back pews, and as my wife told me later, as she and her mother were walking down the aisle after the service, she noticed me and told her mother, "That's the man I'm going to marry." We had never met, nor had we ever seen each other before.

The pastor and his family regularly invited any Luke AFB personnel who were in church for the first time to have Sunday dinner with them. And so, Louise extended the invitation to me. I refused, giving the excuse that I had to return to base and study for a flight early the next morning. Actually, the reason for my declining her invitation was that I was a bit wary over having a young lady whom I had never met, inviting me to dinner with her family. But I did feel a strong attraction toward her.

While driving back to base, I regretted that decision. After all, here was a Christian young lady who was not only very attractive physically, but who also exhibited a certain grace and charm, and I had refused her invitation to dinner. How stupid was that? I made it a point to attend that church again the following Sunday, hoping for a return invitation. And to my surprise, Louise again extended the invitation, which I eagerly accepted. The dinner was delicious, and as I later discovered, her mother passed her cooking expertise onto her daughter. The week after that dinner, I called Louise and asked her out for our first date. The rest is history.

Fighter pilots like to say, "If you are going to do something, do it with style and class." This philosophy also extends to dating the ladies. During our short courtship, I took Louise to some of the best restaurants in Phoenix, and after dinner, to either a movie or to one of the top nightclubs for dancing. As I recall, it was not unusual for me to spend thirty dollars or more in an evening, which in 1964 was a good chunk of money. I was also pleasantly surprised to find out that Louise was fascinated with airplanes and flying. Occasionally, we would top off the evening by going to Sky Harbor Airport and watch the airliners take off and land. What more could a fighter pilot want than a beautiful young lady who liked airplanes?

One thing I didn't know was her age. I just assumed that she was over twenty-one years old. I didn't learn until later that she was a young twenty-year-old. I'm just thankful that, on those numerous occasions when I ordered wine with the meal and cocktails afterwards, she was never carded. Given the culture at the time, I could have lost my wings and my career as an Air Force officer for contributing to the delinquency of a minor. When I later asked her why she didn't tell me she wasn't twenty-one, she answered, "I was afraid you would stop dating me."

With my graduation date from F-100 training drawing near, I had to decide what to do regarding this courtship—end it or take it to the next level. Since I had fallen in love, the choice was a no-brainer. I wanted to tell her how I felt, but I wanted to do it with style and class. So I came up with a plan. I invited her to accompany me to Las Vegas to see the sights, have an expensive dinner, and attend the late evening show at the Stardust Casino, which I remember was the Lido of Paris. We would catch a Saturday morning flight from Phoenix to Las Vegas, and then an early Sunday morning flight back to Phoenix, which I believe was scheduled between 3:00 and 4:00 a.m. Louise readily accepted my invitation.

One major hurdle had to be overcome, that being getting her father's approval for our date. Since he was a staunch, conservative Lutheran minister, and a very big man, I fully expected his response to be, "What! You're asking to take my daughter to Las Vegas for an overnight date!" and get up and throw me out of his office. I emphasized that we would not be staying there for the night, but simply flying in and flying out, and that he could trust me to act as a gentleman at all times. Remembering how I emphasized my gentlemanly character makes me gag. I'm surprised lightning didn't strike me on the spot. Much to my surprise, he gave his approval based on one condition—that we would be in church service the nest morning. This we agreed to.

Thinking back on it, I shouldn't have been surprised that he approved our date. He was around 6 ft.4 in. tall and weighed well over two hundred pounds. He projected a very impressive and imposing appearance. There was no way this slender 150-pound fighter pilot was going to risk incurring the wrath of this man by making untoward advances to his daughter, and I'm sure he knew this. Besides, as I found out later, he had come to like me.

We had a great time in Las Vegas, and sometime early Sunday morning while strolling next to the pool of the Flamingo Casino and Hotel, with the moon and stars reflecting off the water, I told Louise that I had fallen in love with her. How is that for style and class? Shortly after we returned to Phoenix, I proposed marriage to her and she accepted.

My one regret is that over the following years, I have failed on numerous occasions to express my love for her in word and deed with the same style, grace, and class she so richly deserves. Far too often over the years, I allowed flying and career to take priority over marriage and family. I know that this often hurt my wife and our son and daughter, and I am deeply sorry for that. Nevertheless, despite the many times I failed to show it, my deep love for them not only remained constant, but grew and continued to grow stronger every day. And I feel that same love today for my son-in-law and five beautiful grandchildren and three great-grandchildren.

Finally, thinking back on my prayer as a bachelor that God would steer me to the wife He had in mind for me, I realize it all goes to prove the old saying, "Be wise what you pray for, you just might get it." In my case, I'm glad I did.

The F-100, the "Hun." Also known as the "Widow Maker."

CHAPTER 8

RESCAP FOR A NAVY PILOT (F-105)

O ur flight of F-105s was diverted from our primary target to assist in the rescue of a Navy A-7 Corsair pilot who, as I recall, had been shot down in Laos, just outside of North Vietnam. The area was known as one where we could expect substantial anti-aircraft defenses.

Each of our F-105 fighters was loaded with six 750 lb. bombs plus a full load of 20 mm. ammunition. As we approached the area, I could see in the distance what looked like a fairly large group of small puffy clouds over the target area that contrasted with the clear sky. Then I realized those pretty puffy clouds were flak bursts. The defenses were active.

As we checked in with the Search and Rescue (SAR) commander, he informed us that, among the enemy gun positions, there was one particular anti-aircraft site that had to be destroyed if they were going to rescue that A-7 pilot. For the Jolly Green rescue helicopter to get to the downed pilot's position, it had to fly near the location of that gun site. A previous attempt had been met with heavy AAA fire, and if that site were not destroyed, the rescue helicopter would almost certainly be shot down while attempting to get to the downed pilot's position. Other aircraft had made passes against the site but were unsuccessful.

The rescue commander talked our eyes onto the AAA site and cleared us in "hot." I've forgotten in what sequence we attacked the target, but I remember that when my turn came to attack, no bombs had yet come close enough to destroy that site. First, I adjusted the gunsight to the proper depression, and then I rotated the weapons selector to bombs and the delivery mode selector to manual dive bomb. I depressed the station selector to centerline (where the bombs were loaded), selected both nose and tail fuzing, and placed the Master Arm switch to "ARM." Then I rolled in for my dive-bomb pass, determined to kill that anti-aircraft site. As it turned out, it was, at the same time, one of the worst and one of the best dive bomb passes I ever made.

The critical parameters the pilot must achieve in manual dive-bombing are planned dive angle, planned release airspeed, and planned release altitude. If the pilot meets these parameters, while at the same time adjusting for any wind that will affect the bomb's trajectory, the result will be bombs impacting the target—in other words, "bullseye!" If the dive angle is even a few degrees shallower than planned, the bombs will impact short of the target; if steeper than planned, the bombs will impact long of the target. If release airspeed is slower than planned, the bombs will impact short; if higher, the bombs will impact long. If release altitude is higher than planned, the bombs will impact short; if lower, the bombs will impact long.

In the F-105, we usually dive-bombed at a 45-degree dive angle, which made it more difficult for enemy gunners, which also increased our potential for accuracy. We would release all the bombs in one pass with, as I recall, approximately 1/10 of a second spacing between bombs. This was to compensate for small errors in the aforementioned parameters, since given the rapid dynamics of the attack, achieving absolute accuracy in all the parameters on any one pass was rare indeed. If they were shooting at you, it was even more difficult. Dropping a string of six bombs with that 1/10 second spacing between bombs was designed to bracket the target, with the middle bombs directly impacting the target. At this stage in the Vietnam War, smart bombs had not yet come into the inventory. We were dropping dumb bombs, and the early computer systems in the aircraft for weapons delivery were not consistently accurate. Therefore, the vast majority of dive-bombing was done manually. The pilot made adjustments and corrections during the attack to get as close as possible to the planned parameters before release. In fact, a highly experienced fighter pilot could consistently get accurate results since, over time, experience had given him a mental picture, or you might say, an instinctive feel for when to release the bombs. I wonder if this is true today since, with the quantum advance in the computerized sophistication of aircraft weapons delivery systems, manual procedures are probably rarely, if ever, used.

On this particular dive-bomb attack against that anti-aircraft site, I rushed the attack, and in doing so, I failed to meet any of the planned parameters. My dive angle was at least 5 degrees shallow, which meant the bombs would impact way short. My airspeed was at least 50 knots slower than planned, which meant the bombs would impact even shorter. To compensate for these errors to some extent, I decided to release the bombs 500 feet below my planned release altitude. However, when I arrived at that altitude, it didn't feel quite right, so I waited until I was nearly a thousand feet below the planned altitude where it felt right before I pickled off the bombs.

This not only put me much closer to that AAA site, which increased their chances of getting hits on my aircraft, but also put me close to the fragmentation envelope of the bombs. Shrapnel from exploding bombs can reach as high as 2,500 feet altitude. Fortunately, I took no hits either from the AAA or from the shrapnel of the bombs. As I pulled the nose of the aircraft sharply above the horizon and went into a high G turn to avoid ground fire, I mentally cursed myself for my failure to make a flawless attack against those

AAA gunners who were preventing the rescue of that pilot. I had failed to meet any of the parameters.

And then, I heard a loud, excited yell over the radio from the rescue commander—"Bullseye! That got that (expletive deleted)." I fully expected those bombs to go wild. The last thing I expected was for them to squarely impact that AAA site. We stayed in the area to provide defense suppression as needed while the rescue helicopter proceeded to the downed pilot's position and extracted him. The rescue commander asked me for my call-sign, which as I recall was "Crossbow 2," and congratulated me for making the rescue possible.

Those bombs were a bullseye on the target because the errors in parameters had canceled each other out. As mentioned, the shallow dive angle and low release airspeed would have caused the bombs to impact grossly short if I had released the bombs at the release altitude originally planned. And even if I had released the bombs at 500 feet below the planned altitude, which I intended to do initially, it would not have been sufficient to correct for the errors in dive angle and airspeed, and the bombs would have hit short. But delaying release until nearly a thousand feet below the planned release altitude, when the instinctive feel said *now!* considerably reduced the distance to the target that the bombs had to travel and fully compensated for the errors in parameters.

In a nutshell, the distance "short" associated with the shallow dive angle and lower release airspeed was equalized by the distance "long" associated with a much lower release altitude. Result— Bullseye!

As I said, it was at the same time one of the worst and one of the best dive-bomb attacks I ever made—the worst because I totally screwed up the parameters, and the best because of the results. I can't lay claim to any expert mental gymnastics in trigonometry during those few seconds of the attack. It all came down to "this looks about right."

But one thing I can lay claim to. And that is that somewhere if he is still alive, there is a former Navy A-7 Corsair pilot who owes me a beer or two.

The Chaplin giving us a blessing before taking off on a combat mission.

The J-75 engine with afterburner and water injection
gave us 26,500 pounds of thrust.

CHAPTER 9

NEBR. ANG AND
THE LEAD SLED
(RF-84F)

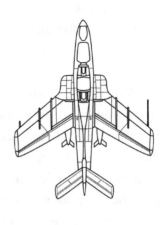

W hen I returned to my assigned Air National Guard squadron in Lincoln, Nebr. after F-100 training, the unit had already received its RF-84F fighter reconnaissance jets. And so, although I'd graduated from pilot training just nine months previously, I was already getting checked out in my second fighter jet.

The RF-84 was already obsolescent when the unit received them. I also recall the aircraft came from a foreign air force, and to say they were in less than stellar condition would be a gross understatement. But Air National Guard maintenance lived up to its superior reputation, refurbished those aircraft to outstanding condition, and gave them another ten years of operational life.

The RF-84, like its counterpart the F-84, was referred to as the "lead sled" because of its long, long, and I mean long, takeoff rolls. Takeoff roll distances of over 9,000 ft. on a 10,000 ft. runway, which today would be done only under conditions of dire operational necessity, were, in those days just another day at the office. As I recall, the flight manual's operating procedures stated that if the computed takeoff roll did not have the aircraft airborne with at least 500 ft. of runway remaining, the pilot should not attempt takeoff.

I never understood the rationale for that 500 ft. restriction since at the speed the aircraft would be at during that part of the takeoff roll, there was not much a pilot could do with 500 ft. of remaining runway.

You certainly couldn't stop in that distance. The aircraft didn't have a tailhook, so you couldn't engage the cable at the end of the runway. And at the speed the aircraft would be at, the web barrier at the end of the runway might slow it down, but it wasn't going to stop it before it left the runway. In fact, that 500 ft. didn't even provide the pilot much time to pray.

Every runway had a few hundred feet of overrun at each end that was rough and not finished, smooth, or clean like the runway surface. They were only there to provide a little more solid surface in case the aircraft left the runway. Therefore, they were not used for takeoff. But I remember that we would request clearance from the tower to use the overrun on hot summer days when the aircraft was at maximum gross takeoff weight with full internal fuel and two 450-gallon external wing tanks. This allowed us to comply with that 500 ft. of remaining runway restriction when computed takeoff roll would nearly equal runway length.

We would taxi off the runway onto the overrun and swing the aircraft around to align with the runway heading, with the tail and exhaust section hanging over the end of the overrun. Then we would advance the throttle to full power and wait until the exhaust temperature gauge registered every degree of temperature that engine would give to ensure that we would have maximum thrust. That may sound drastic, and it was. It would be absolutely prohibited today for safety reasons, but was quite normal at the time. That overrun gave us a few more hundred feet for takeoff, and we needed every spare foot we could get.

I remember takeoff rolls where, as I got airborne near the end of the runway, I looked down and saw the ground crew in the arm / dearm area diving for cover. It must have been a frightening experience for them to have an aircraft at full power so low and so close to them, not knowing if it was going to fly or crash.

I also remember that, after getting airborne in such conditions, it felt as if the aircraft was hanging by a thread on the edge of a stall, which it was. Acceleration was slow, and we would delay raising the landing gear because movement of the gear would disrupt airflow under the wings, and the aircraft would sink momentarily. Once we had accelerated past the proximity of stall, we would raise the landing gear and then milk the flaps up little by little to retain as much lift as possible until normal acceleration was achieved and increased airspeed allowed us to establish a normal climb attitude. In summary, every takeoff in the RF-84 during hot summer months was a precarious, if not downright dangerous, undertaking.

On the other hand, the RF-84 had many positive characteristics that instilled confidence in the pilots and earned their respect and affection. One of those characteristics was that, although it was a "lead sled" on the ground, it loved to fly, and once airborne, it performed with the best of its generation of fighter aircraft. I remember that, on cross-country flights, we would cruise at altitudes above 35,000 ft. and airspeeds of Mach .90 to .92. This was just as high and fast, if not higher and faster, than the normal cruise altitude and airspeed of the F-4 Phantom, which was the newest fighter at the time, and that I later flew. It may have been precarious getting the RF-84 off the ground, but once in the air, the aircraft seemed to sense that it was in its element.

Another positive feature of the aircraft was its ruggedness. Republic Aviation that designed and produced the World War II P-47 Thunderbolt, the F-84 / RF-84 series, and the F-105, which I also flew and have referred to in the combat sections, had a well-deserved reputation for building heavy, rugged aircraft. In fact, the company was often referred to as the Republic Iron Works. We pilots knew that, even if we ran off the runway in the RF-84, we could probably ride it out without injury because of the aircraft's tough and rugged construction.

I recall one incident where an RF-84 pilot from another squadron crashed short of the runway at a base in New Mexico. As he took a ride across the rough desert terrain, the tail section and the nose section of the aircraft broke off. The cockpit section, however, remained intact and undamaged. The pilot opened the canopy, stepped over the side, and walked away unhurt. I give personal testimony about the aircraft's ruggedness in a following section where I describe my first crash landing, which was in the RF-84.

Another feature that instilled confidence in the pilots was that the performance charts and graphs for the aircraft were so accurate that the pilot could bet his life (which he did) on the information he got from them. For example, if the chart for takeoff distance indicated that, for a certain temperature, pressure altitude, aircraft gross weight and wind condition, the takeoff roll would be 9,250 ft., you could bet the farm that at 9,250 ft. that aircraft would leave the ground. The accuracy of the charts was uncanny, and this was true of all the charts and graphs, whether for takeoff, climb, cruise, range, fuel consumption, or landing.

This was of no small comfort to the pilot since the aircraft didn't have all the super-sophisticated equipment that aircraft have today.

In addition, the RF-84 was one of the best aircraft, along with the F-84 and F-86, for the newly minted fighter pilot to gain experience and hone basic flying skills. They were first-generation jet fighters, lacking the computerized flight controls and other systems of modern jets. In short, they were stick and rudder machines that served to quickly build the young pilot's flying skills. There was no auto-pilot in the RF-84, and it was well-nigh impossible to trim the aircraft's control surfaces to where it would fly hands-off straight and level for more than a few seconds. Therefore, the pilot had to physically fly the aircraft every moment from takeoff to landing, which in a short time, gave him an instinctive feel for the aircraft.

The hydraulic flight control system in the RF-84 was an earlier design and felt different than the system in the F-100 I had just flown. Whenever you moved the control stick in one direction, you would feel a slight pressure in the opposite direction. It felt as if the flight control system was resisting your input. It didn't provide the smooth control inputs I had become accustomed to in the T-38 and F-100. This in no way inhibited aircraft control; it simply resulted in the pilot initially overcontrolling, causing slight pitch and roll oscillations until he got the feel of the aircraft.

It was, however, a bit disconcerting on a first flight in the aircraft. And the first flight was solo since there were no two-seat '84s. During a pilot's first few flights in the aircraft, an instructor pilot would fly chase position in another aircraft. I remember getting airborne on my first flight and feeling that anomaly in the flight controls. Thinking that I had a control problem, I radioed the instructor and described it. His response was "Forget it, that's normal. After a few flights you won't even notice it." And he was right.

After flying the F-100, the mainstay of the fighter fleet, I was initially disappointed in what seemed a step backward in flying the obsolescent RF-84. But I later came to realize just what an advantage that was early in my flying career. Another advantage was flying in the Air National Guard during my first few years out of pilot training. Not only was the Guard filled with highly experienced pilots, some of them veterans of World War II and Korea who made great mentors, but the Guard also had the best aircraft maintenance personnel in the military. It was an organization in which, at the time, a new pilot was allowed to do and even expected to do things he would not have been allowed to do in the active force. I don't mean to imply that the Guard was looser or more cavalier in those days (although that case could certainly be made). I'll just say that spirits were high, the pilots were a somewhat rowdy bunch, and their priority was flying. It was a very conducive environment for a young fighter pilot to discover his capabilities and limitations and have a great time doing it. I owe a lot to Colonel Hagelberger, the squadron commander who approved my application for pilot training, and Colonel Christenson, the operations officer who checked me out in the aircraft.

In addition to local training flights, our unit conducted many photo-reconnaissance missions for Tactical Air Command and the Department of Defense. Shortly after I got checked out in the aircraft, passed my tactical evaluation check-ride, and was declared combat-ready, I was tasked to fly cross-country to an Air Force base in Texas and conduct photo reconnaissance of an area where Headquarters Air Force wanted coverage. What seems amazing now but was considered quite normal at the time was that I was sent solo on that mission even though I had less than 40 hours flying time in the aircraft. This would not have happened in the active force.

I had no doubt that the Squadron Commander and Operations Officer fully expected me to accomplish that mission, meet all requirements, and return with the photo products that the Air Force wanted. I have to admit that I didn't fully share their expectations, but as it turned out, I did accomplish the mission and justified their confidence in me.

I remember when the unit was asked to do a fly-by over a certain small town in Nebraska to celebrate Memorial Day. The commander decided that all twenty-four fighters would participate in the fly-by, six flights of four in close formation. I was assigned the slot position in one of the flights in the middle of that twenty-four aircraft formation. The slot position was to the rear of the flight leader with the nose of my aircraft tucked under his tailpipe and just slightly back. The number two and three aircraft were close on both sides of me, tucked in close to the leader's wingtips.

Now I had never flown the slot position before, perhaps the most demanding position in a flight of four. But no one asked, and I didn't tell. I remember working my tail off keeping the nose of my aircraft in position close below and behind the leader's exhaust section, while out of my peripheral vision I could see the #2 and #3 aircraft within a few feet of my aircraft. The fact that there were twenty other aircraft in close formation all around us was something I didn't want to think about, so I kept my eyes glued on my leader's tailpipe. Add the fact that we encountered weather along the way, slipping in and out of clouds (that were thankfully fairly scattered) with limited visibility, and the situation was ripe with potential for mid-air collisions.

As it turned out, we made the fly-by with all twenty-four aircraft in close formation, and afterward, as we split up into individual flights of four to return to base, I breathed a heavy sigh of relief. A twenty-four aircraft fly-by in close formation is a rarity, but we pulled it off safely. All in all, it was another confidence builder on my part, not to mention the adrenalin rush.

I remember when a major in the unit and I were tasked to take two aircraft to McChord AFB in Washington for a week and provide tactical reconnaissance support to the Army at Ft. Lewis during one of their war exercises. Things went well for a few days until one morning when I tried to start that J-65 engine and discovered that the normal start system was inoperative. The aircraft had an alternate start system called the engine crank system, which got the engine started. Then—I believe it was the next day—the wing flaps would extend only halfway and not full down, which was the required landing position. Landing with half flaps was no problem, but it did require a higher landing speed.

Now one might think that with the normal engine start system inoperative and a problem with the flaps, it would be a good idea to get the aircraft fixed before flying it. After all, what else was going to break? The major and I discussed whether we should call off the mission supporting the Army and return home. We both agreed that we didn't want the maintenance folks at McChord working on an aircraft they were totally unfamiliar with. Also, we didn't see the need to call a maintenance crew to come all the way from Nebraska.

Finally, I told the major that, as long as the alternate start system worked and the flaps would extend at least halfway, I was willing to finish out the week flying missions for the Army. I flew the jet that way for the remainder of the exercise and the two flights back home. I mention this to make the point that only in the Air National Guard at the time would a 2nd lieutenant with less than a hundred hours in the aircraft be allowed to make such a decision.

During our last day or so flying in that exercise, the Army liaison officer announced that they wanted to conduct an experiment on the feasibility of adjusting artillery fire from an airborne jet fighter aircraft. Would we be willing to try it? We said, yes! Since I was scheduled the next day for the first flight, I was the first to try it.

The weather that morning was terrible, with a solid overcast about 600 feet above the ground. I took off under McChord Radar Departure Control, which vectored me to the target area and kept me clear of other traffic since I was in solid overcast shortly after takeoff. Upon reaching the area, they gave me a radar-controlled descent until I broke out in the clear at 600 feet above the ground.

I set up a figure eight flight pattern where I would call for the artillery to fire while I was in a turn. The shells would impact after I rolled out straight and level and was heading for the next turn in the figure eight. Then I would call and give them the azimuth and distance corrections necessary to get the shells on target. This turned out to be much harder than anticipated, and I soon realized that I had to slow way down to get the timing right. So I pulled the throttle back, lowered flaps to one-half and slowed down to just above stall speed.

Any pilot reading this will immediately think, "What a dumb, crazy thing to do!" And I would heartily agree with that evaluation.

There I was, 600 feet above the ground below a solid overcast, flying at near stall speed and maneuvering in a figure-eight pattern. If the aircraft had stalled, there wouldn't have been enough altitude to recover. And it's doubtful, given the capability of the early ejection seats, that I could have ejected and gotten a fully deployed chute by the time I impacted the ground.

I finally managed to adjust the artillery fire to where the shells were impacting on target, and immediately called air traffic control for a radar monitored climb back up into the overcast and a vector back to base. Upon landing, I notified that Army liaison officer that the idea of adjusting artillery fire from a jet fighter might be feasible, but it was dumber than dirt. Whereupon, the experiment died a timely death.

In the year and a half that I flew the RF-84F, I developed basic flying skills that served me well when flying the more modern jets. The RF-84 may have been a "lead sled" on the ground, but she was a trusty, reliable thoroughbred in the air. All in all, a grand old bird!

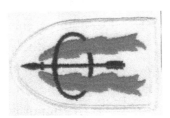

CHAPTER 10

SEAFOOD AND A MEMORABLE FLIGHT HOME (RF-84)

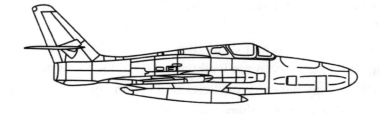

D
on, a fellow squadron pilot, wanted to fly cross-country to Washington State to visit his parents who, as I recall, lived on Bainbridge Island just outside of Seattle. He invited me to go along. I agreed, and we submitted our request for two jets. Since I had just gotten checked out in the aircraft, did not yet have a total of 100 hours in it, and was the junior pilot in the squadron, I would not have been cleared for a solo flight of that distance. I had flown solo cross-country photo reconnaissance missions to bases within a 500-mile radius or so, but this flight was nearly halfway across the country. However, since Don was a highly experienced pilot with lots of fighter time, the Squadron Commander figured I was in good hands, and it would be a good opportunity for me to build up flight time. So he approved the request.

The word got around to unit personnel that we were headed for the Seattle area, and we were soon flooded with requests to bring back seafood from the fish market. The camera compartment in the nose of the RF-84 had plenty of room for luggage, golf clubs, and just about anything else you wanted to load into it, including seafood. And flying back at over 30,000 feet altitude where the temperature is minus 50-60 degrees centigrade would keep that seafood frozen solid. We agreed to make a seafood run on the day of our return.

Upon arrival over the Seattle area, we did a low altitude buzz job over an aircraft carrier docked at Bremerton before landing at Paine Field near Seattle. Don's parents picked us up and took us to their island home where we spent an enjoyable couple of days.

The morning of our departure for home base we took a pick-up truck to the fish market and bought 700 lbs. of a large variety of seafood, including lots and lots of salmon. With it all packed in numerous bags of ice, we proceeded to the base and our aircraft. Since I still had relatively low time in the jet, Don decided to put all the seafood in his aircraft, knowing that the additional weight in the nose would move the center of gravity forward and thus increase nosewheel liftoff speed, takeoff speed, and takeoff distance. So with that 700 lbs. of seafood crammed into the camera compartment of his aircraft, we started our engines and requested an expedited takeoff to minimize our time on the ground. This was in the summer and would enable us to get to altitude quickly before any of the fish could thaw.

After reaching cruise altitude within thirty minutes or so after takeoff, Don radioed me and said that he had generator failure. Since the RF-84 had only one generator, and the battery could be expected to provide power for only 15 minutes or so before complete electrical failure, this was a bona fide emergency and required landing as soon as possible.

We approached Spokane, where an Air Force Base, as well as a Guard unit, was located. Don decided to land there and told me to press on and continue the flight home to Lincoln, Nebraska. This took me by surprise since he was to act as my mentor, so to speak, during that long cross-country due to my low experience level in the jet. But I was not about to question the major's judgment, so I acknowledged with a "Roger." He changed radio frequencies to Spokane Approach Control for his descent while I remained with the Air Route Traffic Control Center.

The big question in my mind was, "What about all that seafood?" Seven hundred pounds of it had cost a bundle of money, given to us by unit personnel back home. Now he had to land at another airbase with a broken aircraft that would take quite a long time to fix. Where would he find a freezer to stash it all in before it thawed? I could picture that airplane sitting on the ramp in the heat, ice melting, fish rotting, and a lot of money going down the drain.

But I hadn't considered that Don was an innovative type. When he returned home, he told us that, while making a slow descent from altitude, he had contacted the control tower and told them he had 700 lbs. of salmon, halibut, lobster, shrimp, etc., in his aircraft and that it was for sale. He asked them to get on the phone to the base organizations and pass the word. They did, and when he landed and taxied up to Base Operations, there was a large crowd of people waiting on the flight line. As it turned out, he quickly auctioned off every pound of that seafood and recovered the full amount of money it had cost.

Meanwhile, I was concentrating on my situation. We had taken off from Seattle during the late afternoon, which meant that the majority of the flight back to Lincoln was at night. I had never flown a long cross-country solo before, much less at night, so this was a new experience. With the distance nearly half-way across the country, things like navigation accuracy, fuel management, cruise/climb procedures, and weather conditions assumed even greater importance. My route home was on high altitude jet airways crossing Washington, Montana, and South Dakota, and thence to Nebraska.

On long flights like that, pilots often wished the aircraft had an autopilot. But, as I mentioned before, in the RF-84 it was hands-on flying all the way.

Determined to avoid any mishaps or mistakes, I became somewhat paranoid, checking the course, airspeed, groundspeed, distance to go, fuel consumption, and fuel required to get home with the proper fuel reserve every five minutes or so. As time passed, however, with the aircraft engine and systems performing flawlessly, I began to relax and enjoy the moment. As fuel burned off, decreasing aircraft weight, I periodically requested a higher altitude from the radar control agency. Since the air density was less at higher altitudes, overall air friction drag was decreased, allowing me to hold the same airspeed with a lower power setting, thus reducing fuel consumption. Eventually, I ended up at either 37,000 feet or 39,000 feet. I forget which.

I felt sorry for those whose only flight experience was in an airliner as a passenger, where there is only a small window through which to view the heavens. Sitting in a jet fighter, with its large canopy, one has a panoramic view of the beautiful, limitless sky. As I gazed around me, I saw in the distance large white cumulous clouds reaching up to my altitude and far beyond, topped by a carpet of cirrus. As the sun was setting, the clouds and sky were tinted by a hue of colors—red, orange and yellow—from those setting rays, complemented by the pale blue of the heavens.

The huge clouds, with their limitless variety of hills, valleys, and caverns, reaching up, up, and further upward, stood as sentinels of heaven. I was awestruck by the sheer beauty and majesty of the panorama before me, and how insignificant my little jet and myself were in the vastness around us. The scene reminded me of the passage in Psalm 19:1 (KJV) that says, "The heavens declare the glory of God; and the firmament sheweth his handiwork."

William S. Phillips, a modern aviation artist, has a painting of such a scene in his book of aviation art entitled *Into the Sunlight*

Splendor. He calls the painting "Into the Throne Room of God." It is a very apt description, and I can think of none better. And again, the line from the poem "High Flight" comes to mind—"put out my hand and touched the face of God."

Before long, I was surrounded by darkness. Somewhere over Montana or South Dakota, I was informed by the Air Traffic Control Center that there was heavy thunderstorm activity in the vicinity. Since I had no radar in the aircraft to navigate around those thunderstorms, I was dependent on the Traffic Control Center to vector me clear of them.

The power and turbulence inside a thunderstorm are awesome and can exceed the structural limits of an aircraft. There would be times in the future when I would have no choice but to penetrate thunderstorms because there was no way over or around them. But only a fool would penetrate a thunderstorm when he could avoid doing so.

In the distance, I could see lightning flashes coming from the thunderstorms, which momentarily illuminated those high, thick cloud formations. This caused me some concern since lightning can strike an aircraft even when it is a considerable distance away from the thunder clouds, and the last thing I wanted to experience was a lightning strike.

I felt a strange aloneness high in that night sky. It was just me and my aircraft alone in that vastness, with thunderstorms all around and occasional bright lightning flashes to remind me of just what a small speck I was in the midst of such grandeur. I felt a bond with my aircraft, which reminds me of a statement by one author who referred to fighter pilots having a love affair with inanimate flying machines. Of course, given their almost callous outward attitude, they would consider such an expression a bit mushy, but inwardly, in their heart of hearts, they would know exactly what that author meant.

The cockpit was my home, and my aircraft was an extension of myself. It depended on me for the control, navigation, and flight management to get us home safely. I depended on it and the proper operation of its engine and numerous systems to reach the same goal. And, I would say that we were both dependent on a gracious God Who made it possible for us to be where we were, in a place much higher and more exalted than the everyday environment occupied by the earthbound. Only the reddish glow of the instrument panel lights and the occasional lightning flashes illuminated the shroud of darkness surrounding us, giving the scene an other-worldly aura and atmosphere.

Then suddenly, panic gripped me, and fear swept over me. Over the nose of the aircraft and around the cockpit appeared red and blue flames. I immediately checked engine instruments and the fire warning light. All were normal. After a few seconds, the flames disappeared, much to my relief. I was confused about what had caused those red and blue flames; however, after a short while, the panic subsided, and I began to relax. Then, those flames appeared again, seeming even more intense than before, surrounding the nose and cockpit canopy. Another moment of sheer panic, and then, with a feeling of relief and feeling a bit stupid, I realized what it was— St. Elmo's fire.

St. Elmo's fire, named after the patron saint of sailors, is a fire-like phenomenon sometimes seen in stormy weather on the prominent points of a ship or aircraft. It is in the nature of a discharge of electricity, red if positive and blue if negative. The area of those thunderstorms and lightning and the air around me were electrically charged, and the appearance of St. Elmo's fire was a natural phenomenon. I had heard about it but had never experienced it. Another new experience in my budding aviator's career, but I have to admit that the time between its first appearing and my realization of what it was, was panic-time.

Over southern South Dakota, I started my long descent into home base at Lincoln and ended the flight with a radar-controlled approach and a fairly smooth night landing.

The reader will have to forgive me for waxing somewhat nostalgic about this flight. I feel a little embarrassed about it because after years of flying, with numerous, numerous cross-country flights over Europe, Asia, and the Middle East, as well as the United States, and including flights across both the Atlantic and Pacific Oceans in the cockpit of a jet fighter, this flight would be considered ho-hum routine. But for a fairly newly-minted 2nd lieutenant fighter pilot, it was something special.

There are few places where one can get to know oneself as well as in the cockpit of a jet fighter. And that is because in that cockpit, all talk, pretense, and boasting—or, in other words, all bull—go by the board, and it all comes down to one basic fundamental thing— performance. The cockpit forces one to be honest with oneself. I was pleased with my performance in flying nearly halfway across the country in thunderstorms at night and also pleased when the Squadron Commander complimented me on the flight.

Although no big deal to the other pilots, or to myself later on, this flight was a confidence builder and learning experience for me. And for a time afterward, this 2nd lieutenant walked a little taller.

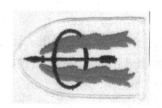

CHAPTER 11

FIRST CRASH-LANDING (RF-84)

It was to be a normal low-level navigation and photo-reconnaissance mission within a radius of 300 miles or so from the base. After I had finished the flight planning and preparation of my low-level strip map, I proceeded to the aircraft, started the engine, and taxied out for takeoff. After takeoff, I leveled off at cruise altitude and on a heading to the start point of the low-level navigation route. I would plan my descent from altitude so as to arrive at the start point at 500 ft. above the ground and on the proper heading to the first checkpoint of the route.

Little did I know that immediately after takeoff, a hydraulic system malfunction would occur that would turn this "normal" flight into a major emergency culminating in a crash landing. The braking system in the aircraft had a feature where, as the landing gear were raised into the wing gear wells, hydraulic pressure was applied to the brakes to stop the wheels from spinning. After the landing gear were up and locked, and after the wheels had stopped spinning, the hydraulic pressure was released to allow normal wheel rotation upon landing.

Unknown to me, since there was no indication in the cockpit, the system had malfunctioned. Hydraulic pressure was released on the right brake, but not on the left brake. Thus, the right wheel was free to turn upon landing, but the left wheel was hydraulically locked. Not even the force of the wheel impacting the runway on landing would cause that wheel to rotate. Only releasing the pressure on the brake would allow it.

I suppose the reason for there being no indication of such a malfunction on the cockpit warning lights panel was because it was so rare, if indeed it had ever happened before. None of us had ever heard of such a malfunction, and as I recall, there was no mention of the possibility of it in the aircraft's technical manual. Who knows? Perhaps I was the "lucky" one to experience it first. Then too, even if there had been an indication in the cockpit warning of the problem, there was nothing the pilot could do. There was no way I could have released hydraulic pressure on that brake. And so, oblivious of the fact that I was about to experience my first crash-landing, I completed the mission and headed for home base.

Upon arrival, I flew the normal 360-degree overhead landing pattern. With three landing gear and flaps indicating down and locked, I rolled out on the final approach and established a final speed of 150 knots. The touchdown was smooth, but I only had a fraction of a second to feel good about that before the aircraft went completely out of control. With the left wheel locked, the tire immediately blew, and the aircraft violently swung to the left toward the edge of the runway. The aircraft did not have a hydraulic nose gear steering system. Steering was done with brakes, and so I jammed on the right brake trying to straighten the aircraft out, or at least blow the right tire in an attempt to keep the aircraft on the runway. It was to no avail. At the speed I was traveling, it all happened within a few seconds. And so, I departed the side of the runway at a speed of approximately 140 knots.

It had rained heavily the previous two or three days, so the ground adjacent to the runway was very soft and covered with mud. With this and the fact that the aircraft was departing the runway in a mostly sideways direction at high speed, the thought crossed my mind that no landing gear could stand that stress. Surely the left gear would collapse, and that would probably result in the aircraft flipping over, coming to rest inverted in the mud, and with me trapped in the cockpit unable to open the canopy. This thought, along with the possibility of dying, all crossed my mind in a split-second.

But, as I mentioned in a previous section, the RF-84 was a tough, rugged bird and could withstand lots of punishment. The left landing gear didn't collapse, although the aircraft was still traveling sideways at high speed through the mud. I jammed the right brake to the floor to straighten the nose out and bring it to the right so I could get the aircraft back on the runway. Finally, the nose did start coming around after I had traveled a good distance through that mud, and it looked as if I was going to get back on the runway. But just then, the extreme stress on the nose gear became too much, and the nose gear collapsed. The nose gear was known to be considerably weaker than the main landing gear.

With the nose gear collapsed, the underside of the aircraft containing the camera compartments was seriously damaged by its impact on the ground. In fact, the nose section was bent. The external fuel tanks were broken, and the engine damaged, from all the mud and debris ingested. With the nose section on the ground, however, the aircraft quickly came to a stop just off the side of the runway.

After shutting the engine down, I sat in the cockpit, somewhat stunned to say the least, and tried to figure out what had caused that aircraft to violently swerve off the runway. It seemed obvious that the left tire had blown, but why? During pre-flight, the thread depth on both tires was well within limits, and the landing could not even remotely come close to what could be considered a hard landing.

While analyzing the situation, I remembered the comment of an inspector from command headquarters who had recently visited our unit as part of an inspection tour of all the Air Guard units who were in the process of transitioning into the RF-84. During this transition, a few aircraft had been lost and a few others damaged, mostly due to pilot error. A couple of those aircraft had been from our squadron.

Our commander had been called to headquarters to account for this to the Commanding General and his staff. Our commander informed the general that one reason for the losses and accidents was probably that the units had received no help or assistance whatsoever from his headquarters staff during the transition that was still in progress. This was undoubtedly the reason behind that command inspector visiting all the squadrons.

It was prior to his departure from our unit that the inspector made the comment that now came to my mind. He informed us that headquarters was not at all pleased with how the transition was going, and that the next pilot who lost or damaged an aircraft because of pilot error could expect to lose his wings. And here I was, in the cockpit of an aircraft I had just crash-landed, with its nose gear collapsed, structural damage to the nose section, external wing tanks destroyed, engine damaged, and the good Lord only knew what other damage they would find. I could visualize my military flying career ending after only a little more than a year out of pilot training.

With this in mind, I did not exit the cockpit immediately, which common sense dictated due to the potential for fire or explosion from leaking fuel. Instead, I sat in the cockpit while rescue personnel and fire trucks sped to the scene, making sure that every control switch, knob, and rheostat was in the proper position. I was determined that the accident investigation team when they reviewed the cockpit photos taken immediately after the accident, would find nothing amiss.

When I got back to the squadron operations area, the maintenance commander, a colonel, chewed me out royally for not getting out of the cockpit immediately. I was then taken to the base hospital, which is required whenever a pilot is involved in an accident, where they checked me over and drew, as I remember, seven vials of blood to check for traces of alcohol, drugs, medication, or anything else that might affect a pilot's fitness to fly.

After they lifted the aircraft out of the mud and got it into the hangar, they assessed the damage and began proceedings to convene an accident board to investigate and determine the cause. Over the next week or so, they took the left wheel and brake assembly from that aircraft as part of the investigation, and installed it on two other aircraft on the flight line. As I recall, they then taxied those aircraft around the ramp to check the brake system. On both occasions, with both aircraft, after taxiing for some time and distance, the left brake locked, and the only way they could get the wheel to turn was to bleed off the hydraulic pressure. The cause was obviously the hydraulic valve in the left brake, which would not release hydraulic pressure when the brake was released.

To say that I was relieved would be putting it mildly. I was home free, totally exonerated, and the accident board's finding was "material failure" as the cause of the accident. In fact, I was complimented for limiting the damage to the aircraft by my attempt to straighten the nose and get the aircraft traveling straight instead of sideways.

My wings were safe, at least for the time being. In the years to come, there would be a few other occasions when losing my wings was a possibility, and I have to admit that, on those occasions, I wasn't totally innocent as I was on this occasion. But those are confessions for later chapters.

I have one other comment or postlude concerning this accident. The Operations Officer, Lt. Colonel Christenson, whom I mentioned before, and who was an outstanding officer and pilot, decided that he should get me back in the air as soon as possible after the crash. I assume that his rationale was to get my mind off the accident and prevent any occurrence of fear of flying or loss of confidence on my part. So, within two days after the accident, and before the accident investigation was even finished, I was back in the air. I was grateful for this and for his confidence in me.

And he had his bad days too.

CHAPTER 12

MISTAKEN IDENTITY (F-105)

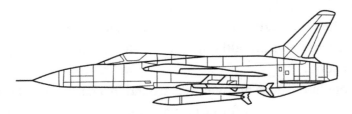

W e had just struck a target in far northern Laos adjacent to the Chinese border with our bombs and were climbing for altitude heading south when we got the warning call from the C-121 radar monitoring aircraft. A forerunner of the current AWACS, it was on station over the Gulf of Tonkin. Its mission was to monitor all air activity over North Vietnam and notify strike flights of any impending threats. The call was: "Two Blue Bandits, Bullseye, 240 degrees, 70 miles." Blue bandits was the code name for MiG 21s; Bullseye was the code name for Hanoi; 240 degrees / 70 miles was their location from Bullseye. I checked our position on the Doppler navigation system, and it showed that we were 240 degrees / 70 miles from Bullseye, in the same airspace where they were tracking those MiG-21s.

The thought crossed my mind that they had mistaken my wingman and myself for MiG-21s, but I immediately discarded that thought since they were receiving our transponder code and knew exactly who we were and where we were. Also, they had their unique, top-secret equipment onboard that enabled them to distinguish between types of aircraft. In the case of North Vietnamese aircraft, they could tell if they were tracking "Red Bandits"— MiG-17s—or "Blue Bandits"—MiG-21s. We had also been informed that there were no other American flights in the vicinity at the time.

The thought of shooting down a MiG-21 caused an adrenalin rush.

With the adrenalin at a high pitch, I searched the sky frantically for a visual on those bandits. And then, lo and behold, in the distance, I spotted an aircraft heading east in North Vietnam. The fact that he was heading east toward the Hanoi area made me sure it was an enemy aircraft, although he was too far away for a positive identification.

I brought the nose of my F-105 around in a hard, high G turn and engaged the afterburner for fast acceleration, keeping my eyes glued on the bandit. As I was rapidly closing the distance to him, I glanced at the airspeed indicator, and it was showing 750 knots. Meanwhile, I had selected the outboard wing station on the armament control panel where two AIM-9 Sidewinder heat-seeking missiles were loaded and placed the Master Arm switch to ARM, which gave me a hot trigger on the control stick that required only a slight squeeze to send a Sidewinder off the rail towards the exhaust of that aircraft. My aircraft's six-barreled Vulcan cannon was also ready, which I could switch to in an instant if needed. In fighter pilot's terms, my fangs were hanging way out, and I was hungry for a kill.

The bandit was descending with me on his tail, and I was rapidly approaching the heart of the missile envelope where the probability of kill is greatest. When I was less than a mile or so behind the bandit, and at an altitude of approximately 8,000 feet, I moved my finger to the trigger. At that instant, the bandit apparently became aware of my presence and went into a hard right-hand turn. I did the same, trying to reduce the angle off from the bandit's tail to increase the probability of kill for that Sidewinder.

With the bandit in a hard right turn, and with me slightly above him, I had a clear top-down view of the planform profile of his aircraft. And to my surprise, not to mention disappointment, it wasn't a MiG-21 bandit, but an F-4 Phantom. If he had made that turn earlier when the distance between us was greater but still within missile range, I might have fired that Sidewinder. At a greater distance, the delta-wing profile of a MiG-21 looks very similar to the partial delta-wing profile of an F-4. However, I had closed the distance to where I was very close to him, and there was no doubt that it was an F-4. I immediately broke off my attack, and he dived away. My wingman rejoined me, and we took up a heading for the long flight home.

The fact that I had come close to firing on a friendly aircraft and possibly shooting him down was unnerving. The question in my mind was, *What in blazes was an F-4 doing in that area where no other American fighters were supposedly operating, other than my wingman and myself?* I never found out! I also wondered later if I would have pressed in closer for an absolute positive identification before firing if that F-4 driver had not made that hard turn when he did. Or would I have fired based on the information given us by that C-121? I'll never know for sure; however, given the fact that I was approaching minimum range for firing the missile, I tend to think I would have fired based on the information I had. And if I had, I would have regretted it to this day.

I do know, however, that I was angry and frustrated over the encounter—frustrated that we weren't able to engage the MiG-21s and angry that we hadn't been advised of the presence of that F-4, and that I had come about as close to firing on a friendly aircraft as one can get. It all goes to show just how easy friendly-fire incidents can happen in combat.

I also wonder if that F-4 pilot ever realized how close he had come to having an intimate encounter with a heat-seeking Sidewinder missile shoved up his tailpipe.

The common combat load - six 750 lb. bombs on centerline station, two 450 gal. external wing tanks, two electronic countermeasures pods on outboard stations, and full internal load of 20 mm. cannon shells. If going to an area of potential Mig activity, two Aim-9 Sidewinder heat-seeking missiles would also be on the outboard station.

CHAPTER 13

ARIZONA ANG (F-102)

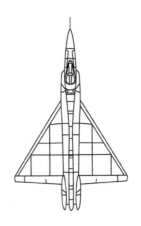

After flying RF-84s with the Nebr. ANG for a year and a half, I decided that I wanted to study for a degree in aeronautical engineering. Since the University of Nebraska did not offer such a program, but the University of Arizona did, I informed my Squadron Commander of my desire and asked if he would approve my transfer to the Arizona ANG in Tucson. He said he didn't want to lose me, but he could understand my desire, and if the Arizona ANG accepted me, he would approve the transfer. Another major consideration in the move was that my wife's parents lived in Phoenix, and this would put us close to them.

With that, I requested a jet for a two-day cross-country to Tucson to apply for a pilot slot in the Arizona ANG. The request was approved. Upon arrival at the ANG base in Tucson, located at the Tucson International Airport, I was shown to the office of the Squadron Training Officer, a Captain Christopher Thomas Hayes III, known to one and all as simply Tom. Little did I know that this was the beginning of a friendship between Tom and me, and between his wife Julie and my wife Louise, that would last up to the present day, fifty years later. It is one in which the bond of friendship has continued to grow despite later separate careers. Tom went to Pan American Airlines, and I went full active duty with the Air Force, which resulted in our being based in different parts of the country and on separate continents. It is a friendship that continues to grow today, with a bond that is deeper, in many respects, than that of brother to brother or sister to sister.

Tom agreed to my transfer, as did the Squadron Commander and Group Commander. The unit was losing its F-100 fighters and was transitioning into the F-102 fighter interceptor. By the time my orders came through for the transfer and Louise and I completed the move (that didn't amount to much since we had no furniture at the time), the squadron had received its F-102s, and most of the pilots had returned from the F-102 training course. Shortly after I reported in, I received orders to Perrin AFB, Texas, for checkout in the F-102. Much to my surprise, I was scheduled to go through the short eight-week course, the one reserved for pilots who had previous experience in radar interceptor aircraft such as the F-86L, F-89, F-101, and F-106. The normal course for pilots without radar experience (that was me) was six months to achieve combat-ready status.

At the time, my jet fighter experience had been in the F-100 and the RF-84, neither of which had a radar scope. My sum experience in using radar for intercepts was zero. In fact, I can't recall ever having looked at the presentation on a radar scope. I imagine the rationale for scheduling me for the short course was that since I had over 600 hours of jet fighter time, flying the F-102 would present no problem. All I had to do was master the intricacies of the radar and the missile fire control system. Whatever the reason, I wasn't about to make an issue of it. As the saying goes, "Theirs is not to reason why; theirs is but to do or die." So Louise and I packed up our Triumph sports car and headed for Texas. I was about to get checked out in my third jet fighter after having been out of pilot training for only two years and four months. After a frantic search, and I might add being financially broke, we got a small, real small, apartment in Sherman, Texas, and I reported in for training. The instructor pilots were surprised, to say the least, to discover that I had no radar experience and was scheduled for the short eight-week course. Their comments boiled down to, "There's no way you are going to make it through this course." Nevertheless, the Squadron Commander took me aside and said, "Darrell, I'm willing to give it a try if you are." My response was that I was more than willing.

Getting checked out as far as flying the F-102 was no problem. Landing the F-102 was much like landing the F-100—a high angle-of-attack, power-on approach. The big difference was that you pulled the power back in the F-102 with that big delta-wing that created lots of lift when approaching the runway overrun. Otherwise, you would float well past the desired touchdown point. However, that delta-wing also created lots of drag, and if you pulled the power back too early while maintaining the landing angle-of-attack, a sink rate like that in the F-100 would develop. Like the F-100, if you didn't correct it immediately, you could find yourself behind the power curve with potentially disastrous results.

On the other hand, getting checked out on the radar system, with its integrated fire control system and missile systems, proved a more daunting task. My classmates had previous radar experience, whereas I had none. The course was designed for them; therefore, the academics came fast and furious. Much of the terminology and acronyms were strange to me. I worked hard, studied hard, and was determined not to disappoint the instructors, the folks at the Guard unit who had sent me there and not least of all, myself. Finally, the eight weeks were up. I had passed all the flights and all the written tests.

Only one hurdle remained—the tactical evaluation check ride that would determine whether or not I would graduate with a combat readiness rating.

The check ride involved conducting different types of intercepts on a target aircraft, using the radar to both acquire the target and maneuver the F-102 in azimuth, range, and altitude to a position where the fire control system could deliver a missile successfully against the target. During this maneuvering on radar, the pilot had to prepare the missile for guidance after launch by activating certain controls on the radar control stick at certain time intervals. Failure to meet the time criteria would result in either an aborted launch or a failed missile.

I felt like a person who had been given a half-dozen swimming lessons and then dropped into a choppy ocean and told to sink or swim. Fortunately, as it turned out, I swam. Not expertly, mind you, not even very pretty, but good enough. As I recall, the check-pilot's comments on my grade sheet went something like this: "Lt. Ahrens can certainly use additional radar experience; however, he has demonstrated the proficiency necessary for combat-ready status in the F-102 weapon system." I felt pretty good about having passed that short course when many others, including myself, had some doubts that I would pass it. And with that, we packed up and returned to Tucson. Louise was happy to be going back to Arizona, and I was happy to be returning as a combat-ready F-102 pilot.

I flew with the 162nd Fighter Interceptor Squadron for a little more than a year and enjoyed every moment of it. The F-102 was fun to fly, light on the controls, and very maneuverable up to a point. With the lift generated by that big delta-wing, you could turn on a dime, which surprised anyone who bounced you in the air, especially the F-4 pilots flying out of nearby Davis-Monthan AFB. But you couldn't maintain the turn for very long because the eventual increase in drag from that big wing caused a rapid decrease in airspeed and energy that not even the 16,000 lbs. of thrust from the J-57 engine could counteract. You had to disengage from the opponent, lower the nose, and dive to reacquire speed and energy, and then reengage.

On the other hand, in a close-in engagement with both aircraft maneuvering at slow speed, as in a scissors maneuver, the F-102 had the advantage because it could fly slower due to the delta-wing lift. Therefore, it could more easily achieve a position close behind the opponent. The problem, however, in a combat situation, was that you had nothing to fire at the opponent with any high degree of accuracy in such a close, slow-speed maneuvering engagement. The aircraft did not have a cannon, and the missiles were useless at such close range. The aircraft did carry 2.75 in. unguided rockets in the missile bay doors, and the pilot's only option in such a situation was to salvo those off at an opponent. The probability of kill was low, but at very close range firing all those rockets might result in one hitting the target.

In short, the armament carried by the F-102 left a lot to be desired as far as dogfighting was concerned. But then, the aircraft wasn't designed to be a dogfighter. It was designed to be a fighter-interceptor, with its primary mission to intercept and destroy enemy aircraft at a distance.

Nevertheless, despite its weapons deficiencies, it was a delight to fly from an aerodynamic standpoint. It was also a reliable, honest aircraft with no insidious or dangerous tendencies, apart from getting behind the power curve as previously mentioned. I had a few emergencies in the aircraft, but none of an extremely serious nature.

The Arizona ANG in Tucson had built an outstanding reputation over the years. Everyone, including pilots, maintenance personnel, and administrative specialists, took a great deal of pride in that reputation. They were mission-oriented and highly motivated, and morale was sky high. The unit was unique in its history, accomplishments, and reputation, and remains so today.

All the fighter squadrons in those days, both Air Guard and active duty, as well as Navy, seemed to have their share of colorful characters. But the Guard squadrons seemed to have a greater share, and the Tucson Air Guard more than its fair share. The stories of some of their antics are both outrageous and humorous, and I could devote a few sections describing some of the antics I saw and heard about during the short year I was in the unit. The unit's pilots included lawyers, businessmen, a judge, airline pilots, teachers, students, and one or two whose activities might possibly be considered just a wee bit on the shady side of the law. But virtually all of them had one thing in common. Their outside professions were a means of livelihood, but over and beyond this was the desire to fly, and specifically to fly jet fighters and enjoy the unique nature and mystique of the fighter pilot's profession.

As I mentioned in the section on the Nebr. ANG, the flying experience of the average Air Guard pilot was normally much higher than the average active-duty pilot. Most of the pilots had joined the Air Guard after leaving active duty because they wanted to continue military flying. Also, many of the senior personnel at the time had flown in World War II and/or Korea.

Two names immediately come to mind: Ed Hurd and Paul Ollerton. Both had flown P-47 Thunderbolts during World War II, and as I recall, Ed Hurd had also flown the P-51 Mustang during the war. Both also flew the early jets, including the F-84 and F-86, as well as many, many, hours in the F-100. I have great respect for these two mentors, as well as for Colonel Morris, the Commander, and Major Wes Chambers, the Operations Officer, during my tenure in the unit. Both Morris and Chambers went on to become Generals.

I remember my first flight in the two seat TF-102 with Paul Ollerton after I returned from being checked out in the jet. As we strapped in, Paul put on a pair of eyeglasses. We started up and taxied to the runway. Before pulling on to the runway for takeoff, Paul removed the glasses he was wearing, took another pair out of his G-suit pocket, and put them on. After the mission, and before landing, he removed those glasses and put on another pair. I thought it a bit unusual and humorous. Nevertheless, although Paul's eyesight wasn't perfect, his flying and handling the jet were flawless. I soon realized that I was in the presence of a fighter pilot whose experience level was such that he had probably forgotten more about flying than I knew at this stage of my flying career.

The same was true of the maintenance personnel's experience, many who had been in the business for years. There wasn't much they hadn't seen in the field of aircraft maintenance. It was not unusual to find a crew chief who had been taking care of the same airplane for years and knew that jet like the back of his hand, probably better than he knew his wife. As I said before, Air Guard maintenance was famous at the time for being able to take hand-me-down aircraft from the Air Force and refurbish them into top operational condition. Air Guard pilots knew that they had superb maintenance support and that the jets they flew were in first-rate condition.

The pilots' high experience level, combined with a more informal, less regimented atmosphere in the squadrons, contributed to their high degree of competitiveness, confidence, and aggressiveness. This is not to say they were not professional. On the contrary, their professionalism was attested to by the fact that, in air-to-ground and air-to-air competitions involving both active Air Force and Air Guard squadrons, it was common for an Air Guard squadron to get top honors. This was certainly true of the Tucson Air Guard unit, which received numerous unit citations and awards for excellence in both operations and maintenance, and continues to do so today as one of the primary F-16 training units for both U.S. and foreign pilots.

The squadron atmosphere also fostered a streak of independence and a realistic attitude toward regulations, which, although to be adhered to, were viewed as guidelines and not holy writ carved in stone. Therefore, if it was necessary to cut some corners regulation-wise to accomplish the mission, so be it. Common sense was the yardstick.

The Tucson Air Guard still conducts meetings and reunions that draw former members from various parts of the country and beyond. Age and the passage of time have mellowed the rowdiness (if not eliminated it). Nevertheless, memories are shared, confessions made, stories told (probably embellished), and camaraderie reestablished.

The attitude is that it was a special privilege to have been a fighter pilot in the Tucson Air National Guard. And I wholeheartedly agree with that.

As a postscript, I'll add one further comment. Remember at the beginning when I spoke of Captain Tom Hayes, the training officer who accepted my application to join the unit and the lasting bond of friendship established between us and our wives? Some years later, after flying both jet fighters and airliners, Tom experienced a very dramatic conversion and a call from the Lord to ministry. He entered seminary, graduated, was ordained and as I write this, he will retire next year after twenty-two years as pastor, priest, and rector.

As for myself, during the last few years of my Air Force career, I also felt a strong call to ministry. After retirement from the military, I too entered seminary, eventually graduated, and soon after received a call to pastor a local church.

I mention this only to make this point. If, during our fighter pilot days in the Tucson Air Guard, as well as for some time after, someone was asked to identify the least likely candidates in this world to become Christian pastors, Tom and I would have been at the top of that least likely list. Which all goes to prove that God does indeed work in mysterious ways.

CHAPTER 14

ACTIVE DUTY AND COMBAT TRAINING (F-105)

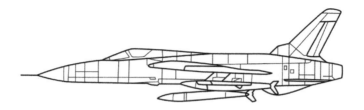

A fter a year of flying with the Tucson Air National Guard, I submitted the paperwork to return to full active duty and requested an F-105 assignment. The Vietnam War was raging, and I figured that if I was ever going to fly in combat, I better act now. It seems that every generation has its war, and the war in Vietnam was the war of my generation. My application was accepted, which was no surprise since at the rate we were losing pilots and aircraft in Vietnam, the Air Force personnel authorities were quite agreeable to requests from pilots to return to active duty for a combat assignment.

I received orders to McConnell AFB, Wichita, Kansas, to get checked out in the F-105, with a final destination of Korat, Thailand after graduation. The F-105s were flying combat missions out of Thailand over North Vietnam and Laos primarily. Louise and I packed all our worldly belongings, which took about thirty minutes, loaded up our new Mercury Cougar, and headed for Wichita,

Kansas. Arriving at McConnell AFB, I was assigned to the 561st Tactical Fighter Squadron for the six months of training to become combat ready in the F-105.

To simply say that the F-105 Thunderchief jet fighter was an impressive aircraft would be a gross understatement in describing the characteristics of this remarkable aircraft, its performance and combat capabilities. It was a product of Republic Aviation that had built the P-47 and F-84. True to the company's reputation, the F-105 was big, heavy, rugged, and fast; it could sustain serious damage and keep on flying. Also, it was an aerodynamically clean aircraft, esthetically pleasing to the eye—all in all a beautiful aircraft from all perspectives. The size of the aircraft was the first thing one noticed. It seemed to dwarf other fighters. As one pilot put it, the aircraft was intimidating, just walking up to it. Pilots liked the fact that they could walk under the aircraft's high, mid-level wing and long landing gear and pre-flight it without having to bend over. The F-105 could achieve Mach 2 (twice the speed of sound) at high altitude, but it was designed for high speed and stability in the low-to-medium altitude regime, and this is where it excelled.

Looking at the aircraft head-on, you could understand why it was so fast at low altitude. With its long, slender, area-ruled fuselage and thin wings, the aircraft was so aerodynamically clean that there was minimal frontal area; this greatly reduced parasite, or friction, drag. Combined with its J-75 engine that delivered 24,500 lbs. of thrust with afterburner, it provided all the ingredients needed for speed, and lots of it. The aircraft also had a water injection system, controlled by a switch in the cockpit. When the afterburner was engaged, it dumped 36 gallons of water into the compressor section of the engine to cool the air for better combustion. It also provided another 2,000 lbs. of thrust for a total of 26,500 lbs. thrust. The water injection system was used for takeoff in hot weather under heavyweight conditions with external fuel tanks and a full load of ordnance.

The story was going around about one instructor who decided to find out just how fast the aircraft would really go at a very low altitude of a few hundred feet above the ground. With the airspeed indicator going past 850 kts. and the aircraft still accelerating, it got too scary, and he climbed for altitude and throttled back. I remember a strafing run I made against targets in North Vietnam when I noticed the airspeed indicator showing 750 kts. and rapidly increasing.

Flying at very high speed at low altitude can be a rough and violent ride due to air density and turbulence. But with its size, weight, and clean aerodynamic lines, the F-105 just cut through the air, giving the pilot a ride that was smooth, solid, and comfortable. This also made the aircraft a very stable dive-bombing and strafing platform, which gave the F-105 a greater reputation for accuracy than most other jets.

Another unique feature of the F-105 was that it had the taped instruments instead of the round gauges for airspeed and altitude readouts. This was easy to adapt to, and in fact, made it easier to check airspeed and altitude during those final critical seconds of a dive-bomb attack. The aircraft was also designed to carry a nuclear weapon internally, and therefore it had a bomb bay that, to say the least, was an unusual feature for a fighter aircraft. But during the Vietnam War, the bomb bay was converted to hold another internal fuel tank, which increased the range of the aircraft.

During its early years, the F-105 suffered a less than sterling reputation and was the subject of fighter pilot humor, primarily because of its size and weight. Its long landing gear and the height of the wings above the ground earned it the early nickname of "squash bomber." The idea was that you could just taxi over a target—tank, truck, etc.—raise the landing gear, and squash the target with the weight of the aircraft. Another nickname given to it because of its size and weight was "Thud," denoting the sound of the impact of the aircraft striking the ground on landing. This nickname stuck with it, but instead of being a term of criticism or humor, it became a term of affection and pride after the aircraft gained the reputation of being the most effective, reliable, and tough fighter-bomber in the skies over North Vietnam and Laos. Both it and its pilots had a reputation for putting ordnance on target. This was before the introduction of laser-guided bombs and other "smart" ordnance. Losses were heavy, but they would have been even greater if not for the "Thud's" ruggedness and ability to take lots of damage and keep flying.

The first flight in the F-105 was in the back cockpit of the "F" model, the two-seater, with the instructor in the front cockpit. The nearly zero forward visibility in the rear cockpit because of instrumentation virtually prohibited landing the aircraft from that cockpit. This first ride was simply to give the student a feel for the aircraft and for the instructor to demonstrate landing procedures and techniques to the student. As the student soon discovered, landing the F-105 was different than landing other jet fighters, especially where airspeed was concerned.

You flew the same high angle-of-attack, power-on approach in the F-105 as in such fighters as the F-100 and F-102, but in the F-105 power was even more critical. Even at landing weight, the F-105 was considerably heavier than the other fighters, which meant a much higher final approach speed between 185 kts. to even over 200 kts. at times, depending on gross weight. Normal final approach speed, as I recall, was around 190 kts. This was 25 to 35 kts. above that of most other fighters. This took some getting used to, and initially, one had to fight the tendency to pull the power back and slow the aircraft down. Also, one thing you didn't want to do was land long, since even with the drag chute, you would have your hands full getting the beast stopped on the remaining runway.

The overwhelming impression given by the F-105 was that of a very formidable war machine, and that it truly was. Just strapping it on was a defining moment. Of the five fighter aircraft I flew and achieved combat-ready status in, I would have to say that the F-105 impressed me most. That is probably because of its brute power, although the F-4 Phantom was also famous for its brute power. But in its element, low to medium altitude and high speed, the F-105 was far more stable and comfortable to fly, and nothing could catch it.

The six months of checkout and combat training in the F-105 went quickly, and I became combat ready in my fourth jet fighter after less than four years since I graduated from pilot training. I was averaging one fighter a year, which was unheard of, but that I was thoroughly enjoying. After graduation from F-105 training, I was off to Florida for water survival training. Then I got Louise settled in California, where her parents had moved, and I left for the Philippines to attend jungle survival training, and finally to Korat AB, Thailand.

One of my last acts before leaving the States for the war was to get my wife pregnant. Nine months later, as I returned from a mission, I was advised to contact the Red Cross representative on base. I did and was informed that my wife had given birth to our son, John, and that both mother and baby were fine. The realization that I had a son finally sunk in, and I was one proud father. And I continue to be so today. The drinks and cigars for the whole squadron were on me that night.

I must admit that my son grew up to be a whole lot smarter than his dad, with talents that surpassed my own. He was a staunch Christian and possessed innate wisdom and discernment that was far greater than what I possess. These he must have gotten from his mother. Whereas I, when discussing my favorite subjects of theology, flying, the military, politics, and history, tended to let passion overrule the discussion at times, John, who shared my passion about those subjects, was able to state his well-thought out positions in a calm, concise manner that went to the core of the matter under discussion. Because of this, I valued his opinion highly.

My relationship with my son, although a little stormy at times during his teenage and young adult years (what father/son relationship isn't?), was always one of love, mutual respect, understanding, and enjoyment of shared interests and activities. This added up to one of the major joys of my life and for which I thank God. One of those shared activities was Formula One racing. His passion for F-1 racing was contagious, soon affecting me and then, before long, his mother. John was virtually a walking, talking encyclopedia on Formula One history, its greatest races, the technological aspects of the cars, the champions, and the casualties. For many enjoyable years, our Sunday routine was church, brunch, and the F-1 race.

The reader may have noticed that I have addressed my relationship with my son in the past tense. Our son died of an inoperable brain tumor nearly two years ago and went to be with his Lord and Savior Jesus in heaven. The way my son dealt with this devastating news gained the great respect of the brain surgeon, the hospice people, and all who cared for him. The brain surgeon said that he had never had a patient respond with an attitude like John had. John's reaction was, "I don't know why this had to happen, but I do know that God promises to work out all for the good of those who belong to Him through faith in Christ. I know where I'm going, and that is to be with Jesus in glory. I'll just get there ahead of the rest of you."

I am thankful to my son for the final lesson he taught me, that lesson being how to die. And I am thankful for the reader's indulgence while I took the opportunity to brag about my son.

I will continue to intersperse my combat memories among the following sections, as I have done in the preceding ones; however, for now, I will fast forward ahead to some memories and confessions related to subsequent flying assignments.

CHAPTER 15

THE "BULLDOGS" BITBURG, GERMANY (F-4E)

Following my combat tour, I received an assignment to the 525th Fighter Interceptor Squadron at Bitburg, Germany. The movers packed up what little household goods we had, and Louise and I, along with our three-month-old son John, said good-bye to family and headed off to Europe.

The 525th squadron was one of four U.S. squadrons in the European Theater flying F-102s and responsible for the air defense of Europe. Since I had previously been combat-ready in the F-102 before the F-105, the assignment did not come as a surprise to me. What did come as a surprise was that within a few months after I arrived, we were advised that the squadron would be converting to the brand new F-4E Phantom. Since we pilots all had lots of fighter time, we would be going to the States for the Phantom's short checkout course.

At Bitburg Air Base, we lived in a small two-bedroom apartment on the fourth floor of one of the large base housing apartment buildings. You climbed 52 steps (I counted them, and so did my wife) to get to our door. My wife wasn't too happy about this since none of the apartments had washers and dryers. They were located in the basement, so doing the laundry meant lugging loads of wash up and down those 52 steps.

Nevertheless, we were immensely blessed by having Jack and Michie Cardin and their son Russell for our neighbors next door. Jack and Michie well-nigh adopted our son John, and when he began to walk, they just left their apartment door open so he could wander in whenever he wanted. John had the run of their place and received much love and affection from them. And we had a built-in babysitter with their son Russell.

Another couple who became a second set of parents to our son John was Gary and Pat Robbins, who reported into the 525th squadron about six months after we did. We also shared an unbreakable bond of friendship over the years. Although my close friend Gary died some years ago, that unbreakable bond with Pat and their children Theresa, Michael, and Becky remains to this day, more than fifty years later. Theresa, Becky, and Michael, along with Russell Cardin, were always coming to take John to the playground or to just let him hang out with them. My wife has often commented that they, and especially Becky, practically raised John during our tour at Bitburg.

Our daughter Linda, my "Peanut," was born in Bitburg, and the friends just mentioned, who showered their affection and care on our son John, did the same for our daughter Linda. Louise and I have always been, and will always be, grateful to them for the affection and kindness they poured out on our children. The military and especially the organization—squadron, flight, platoon, squad, or whatever—becomes like a family. The children of your brothers and sisters at arms become almost like your own children. My wife's pregnancy with our daughter Linda involved a touch of humor. Louise instinctively knew she was pregnant; however, the young flight surgeon insisted she was not pregnant, but simply had a cyst that would need removal at some stage. Louise kept telling him, "No, I'm pregnant!" much to the doctor's consternation. After a time, the doctor finally discovered the obvious and said, "I guess you're right; you are pregnant." Later I told my daughter she was the most beautiful cyst in the history of medicine.

I ask readers to indulge me one more time while I brag on my daughter. She also grew up to be a devout Christian and wise beyond her years. The credit again goes to my wife, who did the majority of work involved in raising our children, not only then, but for years afterward. Linda is a very beautiful lady, both physically and spiritually, and that's not just a father speaking. She also received from her mother keen intuition, that uncanny ability to perceive something of which I am totally unaware. I have often benefited from their intuition, especially in my post-military retirement years as a high-school teacher and later as a pastor. Nevertheless, it has also been a bit humbling at times, since on a scale of one to ten, my intuition factor hovers somewhere around two, and that's on a good day.

My relationship with my daughter, although a little stormy and intense at times during her teen years, is also one of love, mutual respect, and closeness that brings me much joy as I advance in age. I thank God for her, her husband Chad, and their three children, Jackson, Grace, and Maxwell. Along with our other two granddaughters, Paisley and Michal (John's daughters), they are their grandmother Noni Louise's and Papa Darrell's greatest treasures on this earth.

There may be many who disagree with me, but personally, I cannot think of a better environment for children to grow up in than that of a military base. And if the base is overseas, so much the better. Our three tours of duty in Europe while our son and daughter were growing up, ten years in all, gave them comfort with other cultures and enabled them to see and experience so many things the vast majority of their peers would never see or experience. After we returned to the States and they were studying history, geography, or classic art in school, they could say, "We've been there!" or "We've seen that!"

Three and a half years in Bitburg was our first long tour, whereas prior to that, we had not been in one place for more than a year and a half. So some of the bonds of friendship established during that tour in the 525th Fighter Squadron have lasted down through the years. And when we do get together with those friends, which we have done at squadron reunions in Colorado, New Mexico, and California, it's as if those many years have never passed, even though we are much older, grayer, and in my case, balder. Our wives are still the best-looking, just as they were more beautiful than the wives in other squadrons back then. And the pilots and weapons system officers all still have that fighter pilot attitude, even though physically we may have deteriorated a bit with age, pains, arthritis, and so forth. And with those reminiscences, I'll return to the memories and confessions theme of this book.

The 525th squadron was one of the first squadrons in Europe to convert to the new F-4E. It changed its designation from Fighter Interceptor Squadron to Tactical Fighter Squadron. During the three months after I arrived in the squadron, I had time to get recurrent and combat-ready in the F-102 and pick up another 50 hours in the jet before we were sent to MacDill AFB, Florida, to get checked out in the F-4E. The squadron would be receiving brand new F-4Es from the factory in St. Louis.

After I got checked out in the F-4E, it dawned on me one day that, although I had graduated from pilot training less than six years before (five years and nine months to be exact), this was the fifth jet fighter in which I had been checked out and made combat-ready. Again, that has to be some sort of record.

The F-4E was the latest model of the Phantom. The earlier models had no cannon armament. Apparently, the "experts" had decided during its design that, due to the modern aircraft radars, fire control systems, and missiles, air-to-air engagements would take place at longer ranges, and the classic dogfight was a thing of the past. Therefore, since missiles were the primary armament for air-to-air combat, a cannon was unnecessary and, with its ammunition, could be dispensed with and save weight.

The "experts" failed to consider a wartime rule of engagement like that enforced in Vietnam that required the pilot to positively identify the target as hostile prior to firing. A positive identification meant a visual identification. This required the pilot to get close to the target, usually within gun range, which put him inside the minimum range for missiles. Without cannon armament, the pilot would have to break off and reposition himself to get to missile effectiveness range. And what was the target aircraft doing during this time? Maneuvering against our friendly pilot! And what was that called? A "dogfight!"

Wait a minute! Wasn't that something of the past and no longer applicable to modern air-to-air tactics? Well, the Vietnam War proved the "experts" wrong, and the F-4E incorporated a redesign of the nose section with a compartment to house the 20mm. Vulcan cannon.

The F-4 Phantom was one of those aircraft that was very aesthetically pleasing to the eye from some views and downright ugly from others, with its bent-up wingtips and bent down horizontal stabilator. In fact, the aircraft acquired the nickname "double ugly" since it carried a crew of two and had two engines. Nevertheless, whether beautiful or ugly, the aircraft exuded brute force, with the overall impression being that of a war machine not to mess with. It was fast, Mach 2+, with its two J-79 engines delivering 36,000 pounds of thrust in afterburner and instant acceleration when the pilot advanced the throttles. The capability of the aircraft was attested to by the fact that it was the mainstay of the fighter force in the U.S. Air Force, the Navy, and the Marines, as well as in many foreign air forces.

The 525th Tactical Fighter Squadron, the "Bulldogs," was the squadron to be in. It had the reputation of being the best fighter squadron in Germany, if not in all of Europe. Pilots and Weapons

System Officers (WSO) from other squadrons were trying to get into the 525th. Naturally, we Bulldogs took every opportunity, especially at the Officers' Club bar during Friday happy hour, to remind the other squadrons that we were top dog. Looking back at it, I would have to say that we were obnoxious, insufferable, loud, boisterous, egotistical, and unruly—in other words, typical fighter jocks at the time.

The squadron consistently got top ratings during Tactical Evaluations and Operational Readiness Inspections. The squadron leadership was outstanding and hard-charging, both in the air and on the ground, with Griz Wolters, the commander, Turk Turley the Operations Officer (later commander), and Jim Paschal the Assistant Operations Officer. I was fortunate in being assigned to the flight commanded by Lou Tronzo, another outstanding aviator, as well as a strong, down-to-earth, common sense leader.

In short, the morale in the 525th Fighter Squadron was so high it was somewhere in the stratosphere. The leadership gave us a long leash, but they also knew when and how to rein us in without adversely affecting morale. Flying and mission accomplishment were not just stated priorities—they were the priorities.

It has been said that "there are fighter pilots and then those who just fly fighters." In looking back on the aviators of the 525th Tactical Fighter Squadron Bulldogs, and evaluating their attitude, performance, and spirit, I can say that the 525th was full of fighter jocks.

On the 525 TFS ramp at Bitburg Air Base, Germany. The picture at bottom right is of me at 7years old wearing my World War II leather flying headgear with goggles.

A public relations photo taken of me depicting a five minute scramble off Air Defense (Zulu) alert. Taken by a headquarters USAFE photographer.

The 525 TFS Bulldogs, Bitburg Air Base, Germany.
Taken in 1971 or early 1972.

CHAPTER 16

FLIGHT TO TEHRAN, IRAN (F-4)

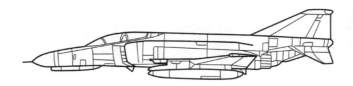

We had finished the short, eight-week checkout course in the F-4E at MacDill AFB, Florida, and were making arrangements to return to home base in Bitburg, Germany, when the word came down that Tactical Air Command headquarters wanted volunteers to pick up two F-4s from the factory and deliver them to the Iranian Air Force in Tehran. Iran, under the Shah at the time, was a strong ally of America and was building up its Air Force with American-built aircraft.

Two instructor pilots in the squadron volunteered to take one of the jets. My fellow pilot and close friend, Chuck Bozzuto, and I, volunteered to take the other one after taking about a nanosecond to consider it. And so, the four of us hopped a flight to McDonnell Douglas Aircraft factory in St. Louis, Missouri, to pick up the two new F-4s.

The F-4, with a crew of two—pilot and weapons system officer (WSO) —was a new experience for many of us pilots whose prior experience had all been in single-seat fighters. It was a bit frustrating at first, having to communicate and coordinate procedures and tactics with another person in the jet. Still, it didn't take long before we gained a keen appreciation for the expertise of those WSOs, as well as for being able to share the heavy workload of a modern jet fighter.

As pilots, Chuck's and my checkout in the F-4 during that short course had concentrated on flying and maneuvering the jet within its performance parameters and using the systems and controls in the front cockpit for air-to-air and air-to-ground weapons delivery. We had some academics that generally covered the systems and controls in the back cockpit for operating the radar, inertial navigation system, and bombing computer, but in the short course, this was familiarization only since this was the domain of the WSO. Later, as instructor pilots in the F-4, we would be not only intimately familiar with both cockpits but proficient at operating the aircraft and landing it from the rear cockpit also.

Upon arrival at McDonnell Douglas, the two instructors agreed to let Chuck and me crew one of the jets, and they would crew the other. This came as a surprise since both Chuck and I had only about 40 hours in the F-4. The normal procedure would have been for one of those instructors to fly with each of us. After all, we weren't just taking a local flight; we were taking those jets across the Atlantic Ocean and Europe to Iran. Chuck and I appreciated their agreeing to let us fly together, especially because if we messed up and damaged or lost that aircraft, those instructors would have been severely criticized for their decision.

Since neither Chuck nor I were particularly enthused about flying in the rear cockpit, we decided to rotate positions for each leg of the trip. We flipped a coin for who would get the front cockpit for the first leg from St. Louis to Warner Robbins AFB, Georgia. Chuck won the toss, which I didn't mind because that meant that I would get the front cockpit for the flight across the Atlantic.

As we strapped ourselves into the jet, I looked around the rear cockpit, trying to remember the procedures given in those short academic courses. I knew how to get the radar online and how to operate it in the air. The bombing computer was no problem since we obviously wouldn't be using it. Dialing proper coordinates into the inertial navigation system (INS) was simple; however, the INS platform had to be aligned to the North Star for it to operate properly, and I couldn't remember the correct control sequence for doing this or the associated indications on the INS control box confirming the alignment. I asked Chuck, and he too wasn't sure of the correct procedures.

I motioned for the factory civilian crew chief for assistance. He climbed the ladder, leaned into the cockpit, and asked what was wrong. I asked him, "How do I align the INS?" I still remember the look he gave me. He was obviously finding it hard to understand that we were about to fly off in this new aircraft, and I didn't know how to align the INS.

After the crew chief talked me through the alignment process, and before he descended the ladder, he asked me with a tone of disbelief in his voice, "Sir, are you guys really taking this aircraft to Iran?" I said, "Yes," and I assured him we would get it there in one piece.

The flight to Warner Robbins AFB, Georgia, was uneventful, and we spent two days there while the depot maintenance folks made a thorough check of both aircraft and their systems to ensure they were ready for the flight across the Atlantic. Both aircraft were given the green light to go.

The next morning we took off at 5:00 A.M. from Georgia en route to Torrejon AB in Madrid, Spain. I was in the front cockpit and Chuck in the rear. During the climb, we enjoyed an absolutely gorgeous sunrise, with the sky splashed with orange, red, yellow, and blue. As full daylight came upon us, we took up a loose, comfortable formation position 2,000 to 3,000 ft. from the other F-4. Before long, we were over the water and were joined by a KC-135 tanker aircraft, which would accompany us across the Atlantic and provide air-to-air refueling for us.

Another reason I was glad for that coin toss that gave me the front cockpit for the flight across the Atlantic was that I would do the air-to-air refuelings from the front. The tanker would stay with us to Spain and then fly to a base in England for landing. As I recall, we air-refueled six times while crossing the ocean. The idea was to keep the fuel tanks topped off, or nearly full, so that if we had an aircraft problem or emergency, we had enough fuel to get somewhere and land. Of course, you eventually reached a point over the middle of the ocean where not even full tanks were going to get you to a landing field, but hopefully, it would be close enough so that if you had to eject, you didn't have to spend much time in the water before the air/sea rescue folks got to you. This was during middle October, and that water would have been very cold.

That flight across the Atlantic took eight hours, and between being strapped in and confined to the ejection seat of a jet fighter, it became very tiring and uncomfortable. Some years later, during a deployment, I flew an F-4 across the Pacific Ocean. The longest leg of that flight was 9 ½ to 10 hours. It was difficult climbing out of the cockpit after that flight because I was so cramped. And that was only one of three legs we had to fly to cross the Pacific. Compared to the Pacific Ocean, the Atlantic Ocean seems fairly small. Later, I could sympathize with those fighter pilots who, during the first Gulf War, deployed from the States to Saudi Arabia in one 13-hour hop.

Nevertheless, as this was my first trans-ocean flight in a jet fighter, those eight hours in a cramped cockpit seemed like a very long time. About halfway across the ocean, and after another air-refueling, I resumed a loose formation position well clear of the tanker and that other F-4. I engaged the auto-pilot, which would maintain our heading and altitude, and then told Chuck, "You've got the jet, I'm going to take a short nap." I could have sworn that Chuck responded with an "Okay, I've got the jet." With that, I closed my eyes and nodded off.

Later, I awoke, looked around, checked the position of the tanker and other F-4, and asked Chuck, "What's our position on the INS?" No answer! I asked again, and in response heard a loud snore from the rear cockpit. I yelled, "Chuck!" With a grunt, he said, "What? What's the matter?" I said, "You're supposed to have control of the jet!" He said, "No! You have control!" I said, "No! I gave you control!" He said, "No, you didn't!" I said, "Yes, I did!" Well, before long, with each of us protesting our innocence and the fault of the other, we saw the humor in the situation that could have been anything but humorous. For a time, whether seconds or minutes—only God knows—neither of us were in control of that aircraft. God and the autopilot were in control while we were both in slumberland. And thankfully, there were no required changes in course or altitude during that time that would have set up a mid-air collision potential. Again, the old saying came to mind, "God takes care of fools and fighter pilots."

After that experience, we decided to take the "go pill" the flight surgeon had given to each of us if we got tired during the flight. We were about three hours out from Madrid when we took the pills. After landing at Torrejon AB, where we spent the night, we checked into the Officer's Quarters and tried to take a nap. But we were wide awake and wired from those go pills. So we caught a ride into Madrid, had an excellent dinner, sampled the wine, and enjoyed watching the flamenco dancers perform. Then back to our room for a good night's sleep. We lay awake until approximately 2:00 A.M., when we finally managed, or I might say, willed ourselves to fall asleep. I can attest to the fact that those go pills really work.

The next morning we took off on the second leg of the trip—from Madrid to the Navy base at Sigonella, Sicily. The plan was to refuel there and then proceed to Incirlik AB at Adana, Turkey, where we would spend the night and then fly the final leg to Tehran the next day. We landed at Sigonella, Sicily, and were told that fuel for our jets had to be trucked in from the nearby town, and a truck was on its way. We thought the fuel truck would be similar to the big military fuel trucks that could service our jets with no problem, even though with three external tanks and internal fuel each aircraft required over 20,000 lbs. of fuel or around 3,080 gallons.

When the fuel truck finally arrived with its Italian driver, Chuck and I, along with the other two pilots, just looked at each other and laughed. The truck was a small, single chassis vehicle that appeared to date from the 1930s. In fact, it reminded me of the picture of the gas truck my Dad had driven for Standard Oil back in 1935. It was obvious that the driver was going to have to make more than a couple of trips to and from town to haul enough fuel to fill those two jets. In fact, as I recall, he had to make four trips.

Naturally, this took a whole lot more time than we had planned on. Nevertheless, the jets were finally refueled, and we had enough time to fly to Incirlik AB, Turkey, and land before nightfall if we got airborne with no further delay. It was against regulations to fly at night when taking new aircraft from the factory to a foreign country because it was not unusual for such aircraft to develop problems. You might say it had not been flown enough to be completely debugged.

Chuck had had the front cockpit on the flight to Sigonella, so I had the front cockpit for the flight to Incirlik. I strapped in, completed the cockpit checks, and turned on the master switches for electrical power prior to starting engines. Nothing! No electrical power, and without electrical power, you couldn't get fuel or ignition to the engines. I cycled the master switches and tried again. Nothing! The aircraft battery was dead. I signaled to the instructors in the other aircraft, who had already started engines, to shut down.

It was obvious we would be spending the night at Sigonella, Sicily. The aircraft had to have a new battery, and fortunately, the Navy had F-4 batteries in their base supply. But changing the battery in the F-4 was a major job since it required removing the rear ejection seat to get to it. As we got our luggage out of the travel pod, the Navy crew chief told me, "Well, sir, if you had to break down here, you picked the right night. It's a big night at the Officers' Club." Hearing that perked our spirits up a bit. However, it turned out that the "big night" at the Officers' Club was movie night. Apparently, the Navy personnel there received one movie a week.

The Navy maintenance folks worked through the night and did a great job. They replaced that battery and had the jet ready early the next morning. We took off, flew to Incirlik AB, Turkey, without any problem, landed, and refueled. Since I had the front cockpit on this flight, I would have the back cockpit for the flight into Tehran, Iran.

Before we left Incirlik, we were told to be especially careful about accurate navigation since we would have the Soviet Union not far to the north and Iraq not far to the south of our course out of Incirlik before crossing into Iran. We were also told to hope that we didn't have to eject since in the primitive area we were flying over, it would be a toss-up who would get to us first—the wild dogs or the bandits common to the area. With that comforting thought, we took off from Incirlik and set a course for Tehran.

Flying over the countryside of eastern Turkey and western Iran, we could well understand that comment about hoping we didn't have to eject. It was desolate, harsh, almost brutal in appearance with its rugged mountains and plateaus. There were few signs or visual evidence of civilization that we could see from our altitude. It was as if the area had retained its primitive state since the creation. And yet, it also had a unique beauty in its harshness. Shortly after crossing into Iran, we could see Lake Urmia in the distance, beautiful with its deep turquoise-colored water. Fortunately, both aircraft were operating perfectly, since this was definitely not an area over which to have an aircraft emergency, and we still had a long way to go to reach Tehran.

But reach it we did! As we overflew the city to enter the traffic pattern for Mehrabad Airport, the sun was setting, and the city was bathed in a golden hue, giving it a beautiful yet other-worldly appearance. We landed, turned the aircraft over to Iranian Air Force authorities, and were transported through the city to our hotel.

As I recall, we spent two or three days in Tehran. The hotel rooms were comfortable, the food was good, and we were able to do some sightseeing around the city. We checked out the crowded and hectic bazaar with its huge variety of wares, smells, and sounds. I had lifted my camera to take a picture of the exotic scene when I felt a hand on my arm. An Iranian man was shaking his head, saying, "No!" Apparently, there was some local superstition about having one's picture taken. I waited until there was no one close to me, then lifted my camera, and without looking through the viewfinder, snapped a picture. It came out perfectly.

We checked out the Shah's residence, and then, on the second evening, the four of us decided to explore the nightlife. We went into a nightclub whose atmosphere brought to mind the term "Kasbah." The person at the door told us that a famous comedian in Iran, as well as a famous belly-dancer, would be performing. But when he told us the cover charge for getting in, which was exorbitant, we decided to pass. As we were walking away, an Iranian man whom we hadn't seen caught up with us and asked us if we were Americans and what we were doing in Iran. We told him that we had delivered two F-4 fighter jets to the Iranian Air Force. He then asked us to return with him to that club. We did and waited while he had some words with the person at the door, after which he informed us that there would be no cover charge and escorted us into the club. We were given a table in front of the stage, and he sat with us. Before long, we had drinks, along with a basket of fruit, brought to us. An overhanging layer of smoke filled the room and the scene had an exotic quality to it. The waiter brought us two drinks which were reputed to be the bar's specialty. I have no idea what was in them, but both of us agreed they were excellent.

The performance by the comedian and the belly-dancer were very enjoyable, although we couldn't understand a word the comedian was saying. But his antics and the response of the crowd were entertainment enough. Afterward, we tried to pay for our drinks, but our escort informed us that there would be no charge. We thanked him, and that was the last we saw of him. We wondered later if the authorities were having someone monitor our activities during our stay. The more I think about it, the more I suspect that we were being shadowed during our time in Tehran.

The next morning we went to the American embassy to arrange our flights home—the two instructors back to the States, and Chuck and I back to Germany. We would have to fly into Frankfurt and then take ground transportation to Bitburg. We were told that Pan American Airlines had a flight direct to Frankfurt leaving the next morning. On an impulse, I asked what else they had going to Frankfurt. We were told there was another flight leaving the next morning for Istanbul, Turkey, that after a day and a half layover, would proceed to Frankfurt. Chuck and I looked at each other, and I forget which one of us said it, but the comment was, "We'll never forgive ourselves if we don't do it." We made the flight reservations to Istanbul, as well as reservations in a hotel in the middle of Istanbul recommended by the embassy person, which turned out to be a first-class hotel.

I remember we had a somewhat scary experience when landing at Istanbul. The pilot of that Boeing 707 airliner misjudged his base to final turn and was widely overshooting the final approach course. Rather than breaking out of the pattern and reentering for another try, he decided to salvage the approach. He put that big airliner into a steep, steep, left turn and pulled back hard on the controls to get back to the proper heading. I had a window seat on the left side and looked down at the ground, which was not far distant. I realized we were in a 45-to-60-degree bank turn, unheard of for an airliner. Not only that, but that airliner was shaking and buffeting from the pilot's control input, the warning of an approaching stall, and it would be impossible to recover that big airliner from a stall at our altitude.

Fighter pilots just assume that if they are going to die in an airplane, it will be in the cockpit of a jet fighter. The thought crossed my mind that after almost 1,500 hours of jet fighter time, a number of close calls, and a combat tour, I was about to die as a passenger in an airliner. However, it was not to be. The pilot recovered from that steep bank, and the buffeting stopped, but then he had to bank in the opposite direction because he had again overshot the final approach course. He finally got lined up with the runway just before landing and slammed that big jet on to the runway so hard that I thought the landing gear would collapse.

While we were in the terminal waiting for our baggage, I went to the men's restroom, where I saw a Pan American captain. I asked, "Are you the captain of that 707 that just arrived from Tehran?" He answered, "Yes," and I asked, "Who made that crash of a landing?" With a sheepish look, he answered, "The first officer," that is, the copilot.

After checking into our hotel in Istanbul, we hired a private tour guide who turned out to be outstanding. Istanbul is a fascinating city, with the Bosporus Strait dividing the city between Europe to the west and Asia to the east. The city is an interesting blend of both western and eastern cultures. It was also very important strategically during the Cold War. The Bosporus Strait was the only waterway from the Black Sea to the Mediterranean Sea. It was a primary NATO objective, in the case of war with the Soviet Union, to prevent the Russian Black Sea Fleet from going through the Bosporus Strait to the Sea of Marmara, and thence to the Mediterranean where the U.S. Sixth Fleet was located.

Since our tour guide had only the two of us, he took us not only to the more famous sites but also to some places where tourists usually are not taken. I remember the look on some of the peoples' faces as if they were thinking, "What are these foreigners doing here?"

That evening we ate at a beautiful establishment resembling a palace where the atmosphere, furnishings, and décor were very middle eastern. We had a superb meal of various kinds of seafood, while belly-dancers performed for the clientele. Belly-dancing, by the way, is not what many people may think it is. It is a very demanding art form, just as flamenco or ballet, and the dancers are highly respected as artists and very popular in middle eastern culture.

After dinner, we went to a nightclub. We ordered two beers that came in very small bottles and cost five dollars each. We noticed a group of beautiful ladies with some Arab men who were ordering large amounts of champagne, which also came in very small bottles and cost twenty-eight dollars each. We decided that hanging out there was too expensive for our wallets (this was in 1969), so we returned to the hotel.

The next afternoon we caught the flight to Frankfurt, Germany. Chuck and I joked about completing another chapter in our memoirs. We finally arrived back at Bitburg three months after we had left for F-4E checkout in the States.

During various deployments, while based at Bitburg, and later when our paths would cross while on other assignments, Chuck and I shared many experiences in many places, from Scotland through Western Europe to the Middle East and as far as Thailand. Whether the subject was politics, war, religion, or what have you, we were of the same mind. We had many sessions over a few beers berating wimpy politicians who committed the military to war in Vietnam but then didn't have the backbone to let them win it, or military leaders who were more concerned over losing an airplane and their careers than over accomplishing the mission.

If I had to describe Chuck in one word, that word would be *intense*. And I could relate to that! I had to laugh when I saw a plaque given to him by his squadron a few years later that had these words engraved on it: "I've never been just a little bit mad!" In all the years we knew each other, we only disagreed on two things. One of these was golf. Chuck was a golf addict and took the game very seriously, or I could say intensely. To me, golf was not only somewhat boring but a form of self-inflicted suffering.

The other thing on which we disagreed was the question of who was at fault for falling asleep when they were supposed to be in control of the aircraft during that flight across the Atlantic. Neither of us would give an inch on that, and each of us continued to blame the other. This went on, good-naturedly of course, throughout the years, even long after we both retired from the military since we both retired in the Phoenix area, and we and our families would often get together. In fact, I wrote a poem about the experience, entitled "An Ode to Chuck," which I read to him and others at his sixtieth birthday celebration. I have included that poem at the end of this chapter.

In conclusion, I want to mention one more experience we shared. While Chuck and his wife Judy were based at Luke AFB, Arizona, he came on Air Force business to George AFB, California, where Louise and I were based. After he concluded his business, he paid us a visit. We hadn't seen each other for four years, and in that time, God's Spirit had been working on both of us. We had gotten serious about our Christian faith and recommitted ourselves to Christ. I remember that Chuck, Louise, and I joined hands at our kitchen table and prayed together. Chuck and I both thanked God for His undeserved protection over the years, for His patience with us, and for bringing us back to Him. Then we laughed at how, if anyone had told us years before that we would be doing this, we would have told him he was crazy. Again, it all goes to prove that God does indeed work in mysterious ways.

My good friend Chuck died of prostate cancer some years ago. I was honored when his family asked me to give the eulogy at his funeral.

An Ode for Chuck

Listen my friends and I'll tell you a tale,
> Of an experience with Chuck that caused us both to pale.

Two fighter pilots in a jet on the way to Iran,
> F-4 Phantom jocks they were with dash and élan.

Accustomed to adventures of going hither and yon,
> They were now to experience the sights and sounds of Tehran.

Blue sky above, vast ocean below,
> Over the middle of the Atlantic, fatigue began to grow.

Darrell's eyes grew heavy and he decided to sleep,
> Telling Chuck to take the jet and keep them safe from the deep.

After a while Chuck, thinking Darrell had the control,
> Closed his eyes, for the hours had taken their toll.

After some time, only God knows the timespan,
> Darrell awoke, asking Chuck "How far to land?"

Receiving no answer, he queried once more,
> And Chuck responded with a loud, sleeping snore.

Darrell yelled, Chuck awoke, and both became aware,
> That for a time, neither of them had really been there.

But the jet had flown on and they came to no harm,
> Most fortunate for they both could have "bought the farm."

The trip was completed, memories filed in mind's drawer,
> Another chapter for each of their memoirs.

But wait, my friends, there's a sequel to this tale,

And to tell the whole story, I surely must not fail.

For over the years, how many I choose not to say,

Neither Chuck nor Darrell admits to any fault on that day.

But that's not unusual, for if you observe with care,

You'll see that stubbornness is a trait that fighter pilots share.

The argument of who had control will leave more years in its wake,

With neither of them admitting to a slightest mistake.

Don't be surprised to discover when they get to heaven,

The argument will continue, with no quarter asked or given.

Until the day when the Lord's patience wears thin,

And He summons Chuck and Darrell to appear before Him.

And the Lord says, "Quiet you two, and hear what I say,

I'll tell you what happened on that long-ago day.

Fools and fighter pilots require my special attention.

For they often act with reckless abandon.

Just as you two, for neither of you did choose,

To ensure that the other knew of your intent to snooze.

So as I looked down and saw the slumber of you two,

I knew that again I would have to come to your rescue.

Now be still and listen closely to what I have to say,

It was I who took the jet and kept it on its way.

I kept it on course and didn't let it fall,

While you two slept on, oblivious to it all.

No climb, no dive, no death-spiral roll,

In my strong right hand, all was in perfect control.

Now cease your chatter and let the argument lay,

For the end of it is this, it was I who saved your day.

CHAPTER 17

DUEL WITH 57mm. ANTI-AIRCRAFT GUNS (F-105)

W e were diverted from our primary target in North Vietnam to attack a group of 57mm. anti-aircraft sites located further north. Another flight was attacking those sites as we approached, and I saw the muzzle flashes of one group of 57mm. guns, and then in quick succession, muzzle flashes of another group, and then another. I don't know how many sites were located there, but the muzzle flashes indicated wide area coverage.

I remember being fascinated at how those muzzle flashes resembled bolts of lightning striking the ground one after the other, or gigantic flashbulbs going off with their bright, intense light. The scene had a beauty of its own, beautiful and deadly. I felt the rush of adrenalin, knowing that momentarily I would be engaging in a head-on duel against those gunners. It was a feeling of anticipation mixed with fear.

Attacking targets such as buildings, vehicles, bridges, etc., has an impersonal element associated with it, even when surrounding gun sites may be shooting at you. It's similar to Army artillery firing at targets some distance away. But attacking anti-aircraft sites head-on gets downright intense and personal, since those gunners' one aim is to kill you and your aircraft, and your one aim is to kill them and their artillery. Many of the targets we were assigned to attack by higher headquarters were of questionable value to the war effort, not worth losing aircraft or pilots to destroy them. In contrast, the high-value targets, the destruction of which would have had a great impact on the war effort, remained off-limits due to the political concerns of our political masters. Apparently, they were afraid that hurting the enemy too badly would escalate the war to a point where Russia or China might become involved. The fact that the weapons and equipment the enemy was using against us were provided to them by the Russians supposedly was irrelevant in their thinking. At any rate, this was all very frustrating to both the pilots and the ground warriors. You might say that attacking anti-aircraft sites was one way for pilots to work off part of that frustration. At least you knew that you were going against a target that was worth attacking.

The other flight had expended their ordnance and left the area. It was now our turn. Each of us was carrying the standard load of six 750 lb. bombs on the aircraft centerline station. I checked that all armament switches were properly set, flipped the Master Arm switch to Arm, and positioned myself for the attack while my wingman did the same. The 57mm. anti-aircraft artillery was radar-controlled, and the gunners had a reputation for accuracy.

While those gun sites had been firing at the previous flight during their attack, I had observed the sites closest to my position, selected one as my target, and pinpointed its position by its muzzle flashes. I no more than rolled in and stabilized my dive, and he began firing.

I mentioned before how one could see the path of tracer shells. In my dive, while concentrating totally on bringing the aim point of my gunsight up to where it was directly on that AAA site, I caught a glimpse of tracers that seemed to be heading for a spot right between my eyes. It's strange how, in a head-on attack with gunners firing directly at you, it often appears that way. In a flash, the tracers passed over the canopy. I wonder how many other shells there were I couldn't see.

When I reviewed my strike camera film later, it showed other tracer rounds going by close to the tail of my aircraft. The F-105 carried both a gun camera that pointed forward and a strike camera that pointed rearward, so you had film coverage to the front and rear of the aircraft during an attack. Unfortunately, there was nothing that could provide coverage to the sides of the aircraft.

As I recall, during the latter seconds of my attack, the gun site I was aiming for stopped firing. The gunners had probably dived for cover inside the gun embankment, knowing that bombs were shortly on the way. However, another 57mm. site just adjacent to it started firing at me. I decided to switch targets during those last few seconds and put the bombs on the site shooting at me. I jerked the control stick to the right, brought the nose hard over to line up on that gun site, and immediately rolled out wings level in a 45-degree dive at 500 kts. I reached release altitude and pickled off those six 750 lb. bombs.

As I made a 5-6 G recovery from the dive and started hard jinking turns left and right to avoid any AAA coming up behind me, I strained my neck to look back and see where the bombs had impacted. To my disappointment, they had detonated right on the edge of the AAA embankment and not inside the gun pit as I had intended. Because I had switched targets during those last critical seconds of the attack, intent on getting the gunners who were firing at me, I had neglected one of the general rules in dive bombing— the rule that once you are in your dive and committed to a known and valid target, don't switch targets in the last seconds unless absolutely necessary, because you probably won't have time to reestablish a new aim point and make the final small corrections necessary for a direct hit.

To my regret, I proved the validity of that rule. After I had made that quick, hard turn to line up on the other gun site and rolled out, I immediately reached the release altitude and release airspeed parameters. Thus, I was not able to make the small, critical corrections necessary to get the aiming point (the pipper) of the gunsight directly in the middle of the gun-pit in order to put those bombs in those gunners' laps. As it was, the pipper was just to the side of the gun-pit, on top of the gun embankment.

I don't know if those six bombs destroyed that anti-aircraft site or not. I would imagine that the shrapnel most certainly did some heavy damage. And at the very least, the detonations of those six bombs probably broke the gunners' eardrums.

And the experience once again validated the comment of that sage Winston Churchill—"There is nothing so exhilarating as being shot at—without result."

CHAPTER 18
UNAUTHORIZED AIRSHOW PERFORMANCE (F-4E)

It was a plum of a mission. The Danish Air Force was celebrating its anniversary and had requested Headquarters, United States Air Forces in Europe (USAFE), to provide two F-4Es for the crowds to view. Other aircraft from the air forces of various other North Atlantic Treaty Organization (NATO) nations would also be participating in the celebration. The USAFE tasked the 525th Fighter Squadron at Bitburg to provide the two F-4Es as requested by the Danes, one for the base at Alborg, Denmark, and the other, to the best of my recollection, for the base at Turslip, Denmark.

I was asked if I wanted to be the flight leader for the cross-country. Again, after taking a microsecond to consider it, I volunteered to do so. The other pilot was one of our lieutenants who was fairly new to the front cockpit of the F-4E. Our weapons system officers and we took off from Bitburg and proceeded to the base at Turslip where my wingman landed. I circled overhead until I was sure he was safely on the ground, and then proceeded to Alborg, AB, Denmark.

After landing, and while retrieving our luggage from the travel pod under the wing, a Danish lieutenant drove up and informed us that the Operations Commander had scheduled a meeting for all visiting NATO pilots in thirty minutes. He was there to transport us to that meeting in the Operations Center. Upon arrival, we walked into a room crowded with pilots from England, Norway, Sweden, Italy, Germany, Austria, and of course, Denmark. As I recall, there were eight or nine NATO Air Forces represented, including us representing the United States.

The Danish colonel welcomed us all, and then began his briefing with the comment, "The first aircraft to take off at 8:00 A.M. tomorrow morning for the air show will be the American F-4E from Bitburg." Now, that got my full attention! The tasking message we had received from USAFE headquarters had specified that the aircraft would be "static displays" only for the crowd to observe. There was no mention of flying, and most certainly no authorization for flying in an air show. Not only that, but at the time, Headquarters USAFE had an ironclad regulation that prohibited any U.S. pilot from flying in any air show without specific authorization from headquarters. In fact, any pilot involved in any unauthorized flying activity or maneuvers was subject to severe disciplinary action, including possible loss of wings.

I was relieved to hear the Danish colonel say that all flying for the air show would be conducted out of Alborg AB since I certainly didn't want the lieutenant and his WSO, whom I had dropped off at Turslip, put in a position where they had to decide whether or not to fly in an air show.

The Danish colonel then went on to give us the specific details of what was expected of us pilots. We would each fly a route over water at an altitude of approximately 2,000 ft. to southern Denmark, then turn back and make low altitude, high-speed passes over the runways at Copenhagen Airport and Turslip Air Base. We would then proceed back to Alborg Air Base, where we would make both a high-speed pass and a slow-speed pass at 500 feet altitude over the runway before landing.

Now here is where it got demanding. Each fighter aircraft would take off three minutes after the preceding one, thereby arriving back at Alborg with a three-minute separation between aircraft. Therefore, after arriving back at Alborg and crossing the field boundary, each aircraft (except for the last one in line) had to complete the high-speed pass and the slow-speed pass, followed by a pitch-up to downwind leg, then base to final turn, and landing and clearing the runway within three minutes or close to it. The next aircraft then would enter the field boundary on its high-speed pass.

Since I was first to take off, it was vitally important that I accomplish all that within the time restriction, or very close to it, since there were seven or eight aircraft behind me, all separated by three minutes or so. If I took too long, the aircraft behind me, which as I recall, was either the Danish Draken fighter or the Norwegian F-5, would have to abort his high-speed pass. This, of course, would affect each subsequent aircraft, and the planned sequence of the fly-bys for the air show would be totally disrupted. After explaining all this, the Danish Colonel asked me, "Can you do this?"

As I mentioned, doing this would be in direct violation of USAFE headquarters regulations, and I was fully aware of what the potential consequences could be. Yet despite that USAFE restriction on flying in an air show, there was no way I was going to stand up in a room filled with NATO pilots from other nations and say that my headquarters would not allow me to do this. Call it pride or stupidity, but I just couldn't bring myself to do that. In fact, I was getting mad over the fact that those weenies at USAFE headquarters, who had staffed the request, had screwed it up and put me in this position in the first place. And so, without hesitation, I stood up and responded to that Danish Colonel with, "Yes, sir, I can do that! No problem!"

When we left that meeting, my WSO, who was about to have a stroke, said, "What are we going to do? We can lose our wings over this!" I told him to be quiet and let me think. I knew I had to let the Deputy Commander for Operations (DCO) back at Bitburg know about the planned flight. That was not only standard operating procedure, but also a matter of integrity. But I didn't want to take a chance on having to tell that Danish colonel that I couldn't do it after all.

Then I got a bright idea. I waited until I knew the DCO would have left his office and be at home. Then I called the Operations Center at Bitburg that kept track of all the base aircraft absent from home station. I got the Duty Controller on the phone. He knew who I was and where I was. I explained the whole thing to him, that the Danish authorities expected us to fly, contrary to what USAFE led us to believe, that I had reviewed all aspects of the planned flight, that I was fully capable of doing it safely, and that I was going to fly it.

I told him not to bother the DCO at home but wait until he got to his office in the morning and then inform him of my call and give him the details. I asked that Duty Controller to repeat back verbatim everything I had told him, which he did. Then, before hanging up, I again emphasized that he would not bother the DCO at home but wait until he arrived in the morning. The Controller assured me that he would comply with my instructions.

I knew that, with my takeoff time of 8:00 A.M., I would be at the aircraft, probably in the cockpit ready to start engines, when the DCO arrived at his office at around 7:30 A.M. and got my message from the Operations Controller. And that's exactly what happened. I felt a bit pleased with myself since I had accomplished two things with my bright idea. First, I had complied with the standard operating procedure to keep the Operations Center at home base

150

advised of all flying activity, and second, I had arranged it so the DCO would be in the clear. He wouldn't know about it until I was nearly airborne; therefore, he could not be reprimanded by USAFE for allowing me to fly in the air show. I had, in effect, covered both our asses. The decision was mine and mine alone.

The flight south over the water toward Copenhagen was very enjoyable, with the coastline of Denmark and the various islands between Denmark and Sweden providing some startling scenery. Approaching the Copenhagen Airport, I descended to 500 ft. and accelerated to 500 kts. for the high-speed flyby. I was surprised to see how large the crowd was at that time of the morning. I then set course for Turslip where we did the same thing. Then it was back to Alborg for both high-speed and slow-speed passes and landing.

Approaching Alborg, I again descended to 500 ft. altitude, and instead of accelerating to 500 kts. as before, I decided to give the crowd an extra thrill and pushed the speed up to around 600 kts. I have no doubt that the crowd was impressed, and probably scared to boot, with that F-4 passing them at that speed and with both afterburners surrounding them with a deafening roar.

Upon reaching the end of the runway, I broke hard right in a high G turn and then hard left to roll out on a downwind leg to the runway to prepare for the low-speed pass in the opposite direction. I had the throttles in idle, and the speed brakes extended, and I used the rudders to fishtail the aircraft to increase drag and get the beast slowed down from 600 kts. to 250 kts., the maximum speed for lowering landing gear and flaps. With gear and flaps down, I turned base leg for a short final approach and the slow-speed pass in front of the crowd. I flew that slow-speed pass with the aircraft on the edge of the stall.

The F-4 had a warning system where if you exceeded 20.3 units angle-of-attack in landing configuration, which I was in, the left rudder pedal would vibrate against your foot, as if to tell you, "Hey, dummy, you're about to stall this aircraft!" I flew that slow-speed pass with the rudder banging against my foot. Later, a Royal Navy Buccaneer pilot told me it was the best carrier approach he had seen.

Finishing the slow-speed pass, I lit the afterburners, left the landing gear and flaps down, and made a steep climbing turn to downwind. I had about a minute to land and clear the runway to meet that three-minute criteria. When I heard the aircraft behind me check in with the control tower that he was a few miles out from the airport, I turned base leg for another short final approach, and when the landing gear touched concrete, I immediately deployed the drag chute. I got on the brakes to slow down as fast as possible and was able to clear the runway just as the second aircraft was starting his high-speed pass.

All the other aircraft in line made the time criteria also, with none more than 10 seconds over the three minutes, which did not affect the sequencing. It had gone precisely how the air show coordinator had wanted it to go. I was told that I had done it in approximately 3 minutes and 7 seconds, and I defy anyone to fly that sequence in an F-4 at the speeds I did in less time. After landing, I called the Operations Center back at Bitburg and told the Controller to inform the DCO that I was on the ground, that the flight had gone well, and that the aircraft was Code 1, that is, no maintenance writeups.

That night, a Danish Air Force officer escorted all us visiting flyers to town and one of the popular nightspots and restaurants. We had one of the largest steaks I've ever eaten and washed it down with lots of Danish beer. We also engaged in lots of good-natured arguing about flying, aircraft, and other fighter pilot stuff. Filled and content, we returned to base and hit the sack.

The next morning we took off from Alborg, joined up with our wingman in the other F-4 out of Turslip, and headed home. I was feeling pretty cocky. All had turned out well, and I was sure that Headquarters USAFE would never find out about my unauthorized performance in an air show. But I had not anticipated one thing, which I found out about when we landed at Bitburg. Someone in the Danish Air Force at Alborg, probably the officer in charge of the air show, sent a message to USAFE headquarters thanking them for providing the F-4Es for their anniversary celebration. Included in that message was a statement to the effect that the F-4E pilot from Bitburg had given a very professional and superb flight performance in the air show.

Well, as soon as we got back, the proverbial you know what hit the fan. I no more than parked the jet when a fellow squadron pilot came to the aircraft and told me that the Squadron Commander wanted to see me right away. I had a sinking feeling in the pit of my stomach. Fortunately, our commander, Turk Turley, was not only a fighter pilot's fighter pilot but also a leader who understood his people and gave them the benefit of the doubt. He asked me what in blazes happened at Alborg. I explained it all to him in detail, and his response was, "I would have done the same thing."

He then told me that the Wing DCO wanted to see us both. The DCO was in charge of all base flying operations, and he was also the one I had told the Operations Center controller not to disturb at home, but wait until the morning to inform him of my flight. Fortunately, the DCO was also a reasonable type of guy. He asked me to tell him what happened, and again, I went over it in detail.

By this time, I was getting mad again, not at my squadron commander or the DCO, but at USAFE headquarters. I was ready to take the hits for my decision—it had been my decision alone— but the reason I'd had to make that decision was the failure of higher headquarters to do their job.

After I finished with the details, I blurted out in anger, "Sir, I have over 2,000 hours jet fighter time, a combat tour under my belt, and I'm both an instructor pilot and a flight examiner in the F-4E. If the folks at USAFE headquarters don't trust my judgment or don't think me capable enough to fly an air show scenario like I just did, then screw it, they can have my wings."

I regretted it as soon as I said it and wanted to kick myself for having gone too far in the heat of anger. I feel very intensely about some things—notably flying, religion, politics, and the military—and tend to speak up at times when it might be best to keep my mouth shut. In other words, I sometimes open the mouth before engaging the brain. Come to think of it, that's a fairly common characteristic among fighter pilots, or at least it was during my flying days. We lived a pretty intense life, and it was not surprising that that intensity was sometimes reflected in our feelings and language.

After my outburst, the DCO was quiet for a few moments. Then he looked at me with a knowing smile on his face and said, "Don't worry about it, Darrell. I would have done the same thing you did."

A short time later, I was told that when the message of thanks from the Danish Air Force got to USAFE headquarters, it could have gone to either one of two action officers—both colonels. One was a real jerk, I heard, a rigid, by-the-book guy who would not have hesitated to inform his superior of my violation of regulations and would have undoubtedly recommended disciplinary action against me. The other colonel was a reasonable, common-sense type person with a real fighter pilot attitude who understood the demands and frustrations that the flyers in the squadrons had to face.

Thank God it was the reasonable, common-sense colonel who got that message. His response was that the whole affair was the fault of USAFE headquarters. They had not staffed the message properly to find out what all the Danish Air Force expected, and in failing to do so, they had put the captain (me) in a difficult position. I never knew that colonel's name, but if he is still living and just happens to read this, I just want to say, "Thank you, sir!"

The incident was closed, and losing my wings no longer a threat—at least not until the next incident, which I will confess in the next chapter.

CHAPTER 19

HUMBLED IN SCOTLAND (F-4E)

O
ur 525th Squadron Commander arranged for a squadron exchange with the British F-4 Phantom pilots from the Royal Air Force base at Leuchars, Scotland, just outside Edinburgh. The Brits flew their Phantoms to Bitburg for a week of operations, and we flew our F-4Es to Leuchars for the same. Upon arrival at Leuchars, the flight leader of our flight of four put us in an unauthorized diamond formation for a fly-by across the base. I flew the slot position since I had done that before in my RF-84 days.

After landing, we were informed that there would be a reception for us at the Royal Officers' Club that evening, and then we were transported to our rooms in the Visiting Officers' Quarters. The reception that evening was more than we expected—a dress-up affair with the British officers and their ladies, with a formal welcome by the Station Commander and other base authorities, along with champagne and music. Everything was very proper and British. To tell the truth, we felt a little uncomfortable with all the pomp and formality, impressive as it was.

During the course of the evening, a Scottish NCO expertly played a number of selections on the bagpipes, including "Amazing Grace." An absolute silence descended on that room, with everyone's attention riveted on that bagpiper, enthralled by the sound, feeling, and beauty of that great old hymn washing over us.

It was one of those experiences that indelibly imprints itself on one's memory.

The next morning, each of us was scheduled for a local area checkout flight, actually more of a sight-seeing flight around Scotland. We would each fly our F-4E in loose formation on the wing of a British F-4K. The British pilot with whom I was paired gave my WSO and me a very detailed briefing on the route we would be flying and the air traffic procedures applicable in Scotland. These included those for entering the traffic pattern around Edinburgh and landing at Leuchars, which we obviously had to know. We would be flying a route that took us all the way to the northern coast of Scotland and then back to Leuchars, and we would fly it at a low level.

The Brit took off first, and I followed with minimum ten-second spacing. I quickly joined up on his wing after takeoff and then moved out to a loose, comfortable formation position, which allowed us to look all around and take in the scenery. One thing I discovered immediately was that when he had said "low-level" in the briefing, he meant a low level. There were times when I thought telephone high wires might scrape the bottom of the aircraft. And who knows? Fighter pilots being fighter pilots, that Brit may have been showing me he was no amateur and testing me to see if I could stay with him. Apparently, he was soon satisfied that I would have no problem staying with him, no matter how low and fast he wanted to go. Actually, truth be known, I was having a ball!

After proceeding northward for a time, the Brit started a slow climb and then leveled off at a thousand feet or so. Directly ahead of us was a large, beautiful lake that he identified as Loch Ness. I remember the scene vividly since it was another one of those experiences that imprint themselves indelibly on one's mind. The sky was slate grayish, overcast with low cloud cover, and no bright sunlight. Even the water seemed to have a grayish tint to it. The scene had a sinister and forbidding quality to it, and I would not have been surprised to see the head of that reputed Loch Ness monster breaking the surface of the water. It was an eerie sight, nevertheless, a fleeting one since we soon roared past the lake.

We turned to the west, then flew south down the coast of Scotland for a while before proceeding back to Leuchars Air Base for landing. It had been a very enjoyable flight. The scenery had been spectacular, and it's always great fun to fly very low and very fast.

Our time at Leuchars was spent flying during the day and exploring Edinburgh and surrounding environs at night. Our hosts did an excellent job showing us the sights and taking us to the local restaurants and pubs to sample the cuisine and wash it down with plenty of British ale and scotch. They even arranged for the avid golfers in our group to play the course at St. Andrews, which to a golfer is a big, big deal.

On the day our group was to deploy back to Bitburg, Major Lou Tronzo and I, with our WSOs, were the last two aircraft scheduled for takeoff. I was leading, and during the briefing, I told Lou to take up a loose wing formation position after takeoff since we were going to say good-bye to the boys at Leuchars in style, with a low, high-speed pass across the base. After we were airborne, I made a turn to the west, and when past the airfield, turned back east for a pass down the runway. I descended to 500 ft. and pushed the power up.

We were each carrying a 600-gallon centerline tank full of fuel, in addition to the external wing tanks. The 600-gallon centerline tanks had a restriction of 600 kts. airspeed and 1.5 to 2 G forces when full of fuel because there had been structural failures of the tank at higher airspeeds and G forces in the past. As the fuel was depleted from the tank, these restrictions no longer applied. There was a program in process to beef up the tanks structurally, but there were many tanks still in the inventory that had not been structurally strengthened. There was no way for the pilot to visually determine whether he was carrying one of the strengthened tanks or not. As it turned out, I was carrying one of the weaker tanks that day.

I stabilized the airspeed at around 580 kts. in order to stay below that 600 knots limitation, and we made our high-speed pass down the runway. Reaching the field boundary, I gently, ever so gently, came back on the control stick to start a steep climb, keeping that G limitation in mind. The jet's reaction was severe.

The aircraft immediately went into a violent pitch-up, nearly standing on its tail and exerting an instantaneous 5 to 6 G force on our bodies. Those unexpected G forces bent me over to where my head was down near my knees. My poor WSO, Captain Ron White, who was adjusting the radar at the time, had his head jammed against the radar scope by those G forces, and he carried the marks on his face for a day or two afterward. The aircraft was buffeting and shaking, and I knew we were on the edge of a high-speed stall. Instinctively, with my head still down from the Gs, I pushed full forward on the control stick to prevent the stall, since a recovery from a full stall would have been doubtful, if not impossible, that low to the ground. At the same time, I pushed the throttles to full power since the violent pitch-up had caused a rapid and excessive loss of airspeed.

Thank the good Lord, the aircraft recovered, and I soon gained flying speed. The F-4 was an honest aircraft. The standard procedure for recovering the aircraft from virtually any unusual or uncontrolled flight condition, including a full stall, was simply to keep the stick centered and push it forward. The aircraft might go through some wild gyrations, but invariably it would recover itself if the pilot could discipline himself to keep that stick centered and forward and not use ailerons or rudder to control those gyrations, which would only complicate the situation. That, of course, assumes you have enough altitude to recover, which, as I mentioned, was doubtful in this situation. Hence my panic to get that stick full forward and full power on the engines to prevent a full stall.

As Ron and I gathered our wits back, I checked on Lou's position. He had naturally broken hard away from us when our aircraft violently pitched up to avoid a possible mid-air collision. Since we were back in control, I asked him to join up and check our aircraft for damage. We advised Leuchars control tower that we would be going to a discrete frequency to do this, and would check back in with them when we were finished. The fact was that we didn't want our conversation heard by others.

Lou confirmed that the 600-gallon center-line tank had structurally failed, with the whole front section of it missing. Naturally, the 600 gallons of fuel had spilled out, and I felt a momentary concern, needlessly as it turned out, that all that fuel had soaked the ground of the airfield. However, even at that low altitude, all the fuel had dissipated into the air with not one drop reaching the ground.

Thank God that, when that tank broke apart, the aerodynamic shift in the center of gravity caused the aircraft to pitch up instead of pitch down. Had it pitched down, Ron and I would have had perhaps a second or two to live.

Lou and I discussed the incident over the radio to make sure we were both in agreement about what had happened, since we knew that when we got back to home base, we would be grilled by both our commander and the DCO, and obviously, we wanted our stories to match. Then we went back to Leuchars control tower frequency where Lou received clearance to proceed on his planned route back to Bitburg, and I requested and received landing clearance. I asked the tower controller to coordinate for a maintenance crew to be available to download the remains of that 600-gallon tank and top the aircraft off with fuel so I could return to Bitburg. I did not look forward to the embarrassment of facing those British pilots and maintenance folks.

But they were cool about it. With that staid, dry humor the British are famous for, their only comment was to the effect, "That was quite an impressive maneuver you just performed." They downloaded the broken remains of the tank. Then, while checking the aircraft over closely for any structural damage, they discovered a panel missing at the hinge point of the horizontal stabilizer, called a wiper blade. Apparently, the high G forces of that pitch-up had caused it to separate. Their solution was to remove a wiper blade from one of their own Phantoms and install it on my aircraft.

Everything else appeared normal, so thanking them for their assistance and kind generosity, I started up, taxied out, and took off for the return flight to Bitburg. Upon arrival at the squadron, I discovered that Lou and his WSO, along with the Squadron Commander, the Operations Officer, and the Wing DCO were waiting for us in the squadron lounge.

Lou and I both gave our versions of the event that we discussed in the air over Leuchars. Our WSOs agreed with our stories. Everything we said was true, although I must admit that we left out a few critical details, such as the high-speed fly-by. Lou said that when he had last glanced at the airspeed indicator while flying formation before the tank came apart, it indicated somewhere around 400 kts. And I allowed as how the airspeed was probably a bit higher than that when the tank separated, but I didn't specify how much higher. We both emphasized the fact that the tank had failed below the operating restrictions specified in the aircraft technical manual. The fact that there had been previous failures of the tank in F-4 units around the world weighed in our favor.

We could tell by the DCO's facial expressions that he suspected we were holding back some details. He probably suspected that the incident had occurred during a high-speed pass. But it was also obvious that he didn't want to take a chance on Lou and me getting into trouble with higher headquarters, so he was not going to press it. As I recall, Lou was an Assistant Operations Officer of the squadron at the time, and I was a Flight Commander. The DCO thought highly of both of us and our contributions to the Wing's mission as both instructor pilots and staff officers. And that's no brag, just fact!

The DCO looked both of us in the eyes for a few moments, then laughed to let us know he knew we were "blowing smoke." While smiling, he said, "You're both a couple of lousy liars" and told us to get out of there and get back to work.

Headquarters USAFE was informed of the failure of the 600-gallon tank, which regulations demanded. But the possibility of its failure being due to a high-speed pass never was mentioned, only the fact that it had failed below the flight restrictions specified in the technical manual. The last thing I needed was for headquarters to learn I had made an unauthorized high-speed fly-by in Scotland, resulting in that tank failure—and that coming on the heels of flying an unauthorized air show in Denmark, as described in the previous chapter. That could have been hazardous to my flying career.

All in all, it was a very humbling experience for me. But again, the good Lord looks out for fools and fighter pilots. I had dodged another bullet, and my wings were safe again—for the time being.

CHAPTER 20

TEST HOP (F-4)

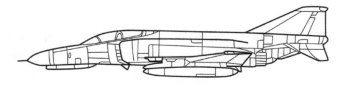

As an F-4E instructor pilot and flight examiner, I was also put on orders as a Functional Check Flight (FCF) pilot. Every aircraft—after receiving major maintenance on the engines, flight controls, fuel systems, hydraulic systems, electrical systems, and other critical aircraft components and systems—had to have a test flight to ensure everything worked as advertised before being released to the flight line for normal operations. The FCF pilots and Weapon System Officers conducted those test flights.

I really enjoyed those flights, as did all the FCF crews. Why? Because during those test flights, you were required to do things with the aircraft that you otherwise would seldom do during normal operations. You usually checked out all the primary systems, not just the system that had undergone major maintenance. And you weren't gentle about it. The objective was that, if a system was going to malfunction or fail, you wanted it to do so during that test flight and not when some young lieutenant with minimum experience in the jet was flying it at night, in the weather, or in other similarly demanding conditions. And so, you were a bit more demanding than usual when testing the jet's various systems and components.

In other words, test flights were very aggressive, flown with the jet in a clean configuration without any external fuel tanks or other stores.

Flying the jet clean in and of itself was a rush for the pilot since he could get maximum performance. Test flights were usually of short duration. Normal flight time for a test flight was 30 minutes or so because much of the flight was at high power settings and with afterburners, causing those 12,000 lbs. of internal fuel to burn at a rapid rate.

During the testing, unusually hard and rapid inputs were made to the flight controls in pitch, roll, and yaw to ensure that the hydraulic flight controls responded immediately and correctly; and, furthermore, that the stability augmentation system, designed to dampen out any aircraft oscillations and provide dynamic stability, operated as designed. Rapid throttle bursts jammed the throttles from idle to 100 percent power and then full afterburner to ensure that the engine fuel controls and computer provided smooth and rapid acceleration within the required few seconds without any compressor stalls or other malfunctions. You flew the aircraft into full stalls, both slow speed stalls and accelerated stalls, to test whether it was giving you proper stall indications and whether it would recover promptly with the correct recovery techniques.

But the highlight of the test flight was the Mach run. You took the aircraft to high altitude—40,000 ft. or above—and ran it out to see how fast it would go. You were looking to achieve a speed of Mach 2.0 (twice the speed of sound) since the jet was designed to go Mach 2.0 and could actually fly even slightly faster—that is, until various modifications had increased the weight of the aircraft, which of course affected its top speed. Rarely, if ever, during normal flight operations or even in combat, did you fly the aircraft at these speeds, so being able to do so on a functional test flight was something of a treat.

One day, while my WSO and I were conducting a functional check flight, and after I had completed all other checks, I climbed to 40,000 ft. and prepared for the Mach run. Checking engine instruments and fuel status, I advanced the throttles to full 100 percent military power and quickly accelerated to Mach .95. I then shoved both throttles into afterburner and felt the kick in the pants as they lit, and the tremendous acceleration provided by those afterburners as the engines were now giving me 36,000 lbs. of thrust. With both engines in afterburner, fuel was flowing to the engines at the rate of around 40,000 lbs/hr. We were passing through the transonic region, rapidly approaching Mach 1.0, the speed of sound. The jet was becoming more and more sensitive in this region. A few moments later, I saw that the Mach meter was indicating Mach 1.0. At the same time, I noticed the needles on the pressure instruments—the altimeter and vertical velocity indicator that measure atmospheric pressure—jump erratically across the face of the instruments due to the drastic change in pressure caused by the shock wave forming on the aircraft as we reached the speed of sound. The instruments immediately resumed normal operation after we reached supersonic speed.

The jet was now extremely sensitive to any control input, I had to treat her with tenderness and finesse, avoiding any rough or abrupt control movements, if she was to reach the peak we were both striving for. With my right hand softly resting on the jet's controls between my legs, I firmly, but slowly and gently, applied the necessary pressure inputs to steady her and hold her in position as her performance in speed and intensity increased.

My left hand maintained forward pressure on her throttles to provide the maximum thrust that would allow her to give me all that she had to give.

Before long, she had taken us to Mach 1.5, and she was still accelerating toward the goal we both wanted to reach and that was drawing closer. With my thumb resting on her trim button, I made the small pressure inputs to keep her straight and level, ever so careful not to over control, which could cause her to go wild and take us both over the edge. Our airspeed was well over a thousand miles per hour. I sensed her speaking to me when I felt her shudder as the tremendous force of that airstream with a wind of a dozen hurricanes enveloped, embraced, and caressed her shapely form, and penetrated her engine bay inner recesses. And I was speaking to her, urging her on, "That's it, darling, Go for it! Go for it!" She was straining to reach the peak and give me all that she was capable of giving.

Fuel was getting low, and I knew that I would have to discontinue the Mach run shortly. But I didn't want to pull the reins on her quite yet, so I let her go for it. She was responding beautifully to my gentle touch as I urged her on. Finally, between Mach 1.90 and 1.95, at approximately 1,250 miles per hour, with her still accelerating, I had to rein her in and discontinue the run or I would be recovering back at home base with an emergency fuel state.

I ever so slowly pulled the throttles out of afterburner and then decided to see how high she would take me with all that excess airspeed. I was shooting for 60,000 ft. or higher. I passed 50,000 ft., then 55,000 ft., still climbing. Then I noticed something strange and unique and which I distinctly remember to this day. Looking toward the horizon, I could see what appeared to be the slight curvature of the earth. Also, the sky at that altitude took on a different hue and vivid color, an intense blue, before the blackness of space. Above most of the atmosphere and its pollution, the sky was cleaner, brighter, and clearer. It is hard to describe, but it was something that definitely made an indelible imprint on my senses. I felt pity for the earthbound and was thankful to God for allowing me to do what I was doing, to see what I was seeing, and to experience what I was experiencing.

Then I remembered that flight above 50,000 ft. altitude was restricted by regulation unless you were wearing a full pressure suit, such as the astronauts wear. And for good reason! Above that altitude, if you lost cockpit pressurization, which was not an unknown occurrence in the F-4, and you weren't wearing a full pressure suit (which I was not), there was not enough atmospheric pressure to keep the blood flowing in your arteries and veins. In other words, the blood just stagnated and bubbled. The physiological term for this was "blood boiling." Obviously, the result was a quick death, and probably not a very pleasant one at that.

I wasn't quite to 60,000 ft., but fuel in the jet was now critical, so I decided to call it a day. I rolled her over, inverted, and with a gentle touch, brought her down from the heights to which she had taken us. Once below 50,000 ft., I put her into a slow, lazy descent with throttles well back to conserve fuel, and returned to base. I can only imagine the indescribable thrill those X-15 pilots must have felt who flew that research rocket aircraft to speeds of well over 4,000 miles per hour and into space at altitudes of over 165,000 ft. Compared to that, my experience would be pretty ho-hum. Nevertheless, I still remember the view at that altitude and the feelings I experienced during the test hop that day.

I have never smoked a joint, sniffed cocaine, or experimented with any illegal drug. I never even felt the slightest desire to do so. After all, no such rush could ever match the rush of strapping on a supersonic jet fighter, taking her to the highest heavens, and flying her to her maximum performance capability, going where few go, seeing what few see, and experiencing what few experience.

As I recall, I did land from that flight with my fuel state at the emergency level.

CHAPTER 21

ONE VERY BIG BANG
(F-105)

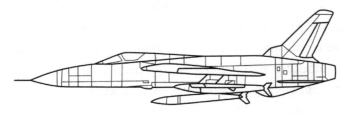

We had bombed our primary target and were directed to an area where the latest intelligence indicated there was a large enemy ammunition storage depot located in the vicinity. Destroying such a target was a high priority. However, the intelligence folks had not been able to pinpoint its exact location. We were asked to spray the area with 20mm. cannon fire in the hope that a few of those shells might hit that ammo dump. The cannon shells we were carrying were high-explosive and incendiary, so it wouldn't take many shells to set off that stored ammunition.

That day, I was flying an F-105F model, one of the two-seaters, instead of the single seat F-105D. Apparently, the maintenance folks had not been able to provide enough D models for all the scheduled missions and had to draw on the F models to fulfill our tasking from higher headquarters. I was alone in the aircraft, with the backseat empty.

The F model I was flying, however, was one of the few two-seaters on base that had the rear cockpit modified to incorporate some new "cosmic" top- secret electronic equipment. I forget what exactly that equipment was designed for, but as I recall, it had something to do with monitoring North Vietnamese communications. Be that as it may, because of the sensitive nature of that equipment, pilots were restricted from strafing with those F models that had been modified. The reason for the restriction on strafing was because of the higher probability of being hit by ground fire, and the powers that be obviously didn't want to take any chances on losing any of those modified F models.

The probability of being hit while strafing increased dramatically when conducting low-angle strafing, since you had to get much closer to the target at a much lower altitude before firing to achieve a reasonable degree of assurance that you would hit what you were shooting at. Due to this high probability of being hit, low-angle strafing was forbidden over North Vietnam. Only high-angle strafing was allowed. High angle strafing made it more difficult for those gunners on the ground because you were firing at a longer range and higher altitude. Nevertheless, the fact that the range of those AAA guns was greater than the range of the aircraft's cannon meant that, whether strafing from a low angle or a high angle, those gunners were able to fire at you before you got into range to fire at them. I remember reading that in World War II, the aircraft loss rate from strafing was four times greater than the loss rate from air-to-air combat.

As I mentioned in a previous section, strafing is one of the fighter pilot's favorite activities. The sound and vibration of that cannon spewing out 20mm. shells and leaving tracer trails behind them, and the flashes of those shells hitting the target and plowing up the ground all around it, create quite a feeling of power and get the adrenalin flowing. In short, it's quite a rush.

My wingman was flying an F-105D and was cleared for strafing, while I, on the other hand, was restricted from doing so in that modified F-105F. Yet, two aircraft strafing could cover more area. Then, to show how fighter pilots think, I rationalized. It was combat, I was in a jet fighter loaded with 20mm. ammunition, and there was a target to strafe. It took me only a few seconds to decide what to do. I would strafe, but I would use discretion and do high-angle strafing only. But before doing so, I had to consider another matter, that being the gun camera.

Whenever bombs, missiles, rockets, cannons, etc., were released or fired from the aircraft, the gun camera was automatically activated to film the path of the ordnance and impact point. The film was downloaded and reviewed by specialists after every mission, and anything of special interest was brought to the attention of the intelligence folks, as well as to higher authorities. The gun camera film was titled with the pilot's name, squadron, and aircraft tail number. Obviously, I didn't want the fact that I had strafed with this aircraft documented on film.

No problem! I reached back to the circuit breaker panel, located the gun camera circuit breaker, and pulled it out. This prevented electrical power from getting to the gun camera, thereby rendering it inoperative.

With that, I positioned myself for the strafing pass and rolled in. My dive angle was around 30 degrees, and I began firing at approximately a 3,000 ft. altitude. As I noted in a previous section, that six-barreled Vulcan Gatling gun in the aircraft spewed out a hundred cannon shells a second, and it was so accurate the pilots joked about being able to thread a needle with it. That was great when attacking a pinpoint target, but for an area target such as the one we were attacking, you needed more of a spread with those shells to cover a larger area. So, to get that spread, I kicked the rudder pedals to swing the nose back and forth while firing. With its high rate of fire of 100 shells a second, the sound of that Vulcan cannon was different from that of normal cannon fire. All you heard was a constant br-r-r-r-r-r-r.

After firing a three-second burst, which equated to 300 cannon shells, I released the trigger and hauled back on the stick to recover from the dive. I was pulling hard to get the nose of the aircraft up to the horizon when I encountered massive turbulence, so violent that it flipped the aircraft over into an inverted position. There I was, on my back, looking at the ground that appeared very, very close since I had not fully recovered from my dive at the time. In a panic, I applied the full left aileron and jammed the left rudder to the floor to roll the aircraft upright so I could climb for altitude. The violent maneuvering had caused a substantial loss of airspeed, so I shoved the power to the maximum to get the thrust needed to accelerate.

As I started a climbing turn and looked out to the right and back, the cause for that massive turbulence that flipped me over became clear. My cannon shells had found that ammunition dump, and the shock wave from the tremendous explosion had hit my aircraft as I was recovering from the strafing pass. It was so strong it flipped me inverted.

In the short time it had taken me to recover and start my climb, perhaps ten seconds or so, the smoke column of that massive explosion had reached between 3,000 to 5,000 ft. in altitude. My wingman, who had rolled in for his strafing pass shortly after I did, and was in his dive when the ammo dump went up, told me later that the fireball looked like a mini nuclear bomb going off. He immediately aborted his pass and figured that I had been caught in that fireball and was dead. Then, he told me, much to his surprise, he saw through the smoke column an aircraft clawing for altitude and knew I was alive.

Those cannon shells found that ammo dump by pure chance. After all, it doesn't take a lot of talent to spray the ground with cannon fire. Nevertheless, my wingman and I were pleased with ourselves and what we considered good mission results as we joined up, climbed out of the area, and headed for home.

I don't remember what exactly we told the intelligence debriefers. We claimed the ammo dump destroyed, and obviously my wingman got credit for it since I wasn't about to admit that I strafed in that F model. But it wasn't on his camera film. What I'm sure he did was tell the debriefers that his camera malfunctioned during the mission and failed to record his strafing pass. At any rate, there was no further inquiry.

Looking back on it, I have often regretted pulling that gun camera circuit breaker and not taking my chances on my violation not being noticed. Then too, even if it had been noticed, perhaps I would not have been reprimanded for strafing because of the results obtained. I would really have liked to have that ammo dump going up in a huge fireball on film. Even today, when I see World War II films of P-38s, P-47s, and P-51s strafing targets followed by huge explosions, I think back on blowing up that ammo dump.

But then again, maybe it's best I did pull that circuit breaker since the film would have shown I was clearly guilty of violating a standard operating restriction. And who knows what that may have led to as far as my flying career was concerned, given the atmosphere that prevailed at the time. It was a time when everyone, especially the higher-ups, were walking on eggshells due to the political and operational restrictions placed on us.

One thing, however, is for certain. It was a very, very big bang.

CHAPTER 22

SECOND CRASH LANDING (F-4E)

W hile assigned to George Air Force Base, California, I was both an instructor pilot and Chief of the Weapons and Tactics Division of the 35th Tactical Fighter Wing. One of the many programs run out of my office was the renovation and modernization of our tactical bombing and gunnery ranges, a program that higher headquarters had ordered for all the tactical ranges throughout the country. This was a high priority program whose goal was to have the ranges reflect a more current target and threat environment for the pilots. In this capacity, I was scheduled to take an F-4 and fly to 12th Air Force Headquarters, located at Bergstrom AFB in Austin, Texas, to brief the three-star commanding general on the plan my folks and I had developed to implement the program.

Charley Rose, another pilot in the Wing, went with me to help with the briefing. Since I outranked him, I gave him the back cockpit and I took the front cockpit of the jet.

The briefing at 12 AF headquarters went well, the general seemed pleased, and his staff complimented me on the presentation. Charley and I planned to fly back to George AFB the next day. Since we wanted to get some nighttime to help fulfill our semi-annual requirement for night flying, we decided to delay takeoff the next day until later in the afternoon. Then we would fly to Luke

AFB, Arizona, land and take on fuel, and then after nightfall, fly a long, circuitous navigation route back to George AFB.

While at 12AF headquarters, we met some other fighter pilots who were there to give briefings too, as well as old friends working at headquarters whom we had served with in the past. We visiting pilots were all staying in the same hotel where the Air Force had contracted rooms, and some of us arranged to have dinner together. After a late dinner, a group of us gathered together in the room of one of the pilots. Fighter pilots being fighter pilots, we were soon engaged in loud, boisterous discussion (perhaps argument is a better word) involving airplanes, flying, our political and military leaders, and other issues important to the fighter pilot community. Each of us, as self-designated "experts," had the solutions to the problems facing the country, the military, and our individual units. Along with our loud discussion and camaraderie, we were enjoying the company of Jack Daniels, Johnny Walker, and Mr. Heineken.

Since Charley and I weren't taking off the next day until in the afternoon, we weren't in any hurry to leave the party. I don't remember what time it finally broke up, but I do know it was in the wee hours of the morning. I think we finally got to bed around 5:00 A.M.

The next day, we took off around 2:00 P.M. en route to Luke AFB, arriving there just short of two hours later. I entered a three-mile initial leg and pitched out for a 360-degree overhead pattern and landing. Rolling out on downwind leg, I put the landing gear down and immediately got a "check hydraulics" light on the warning lights panel. Doing so, I discovered that the utility hydraulic system gauge, which normally indicates 3,000 psi pressure, was showing zero pressure. I had lost the utility hydraulic system. The emergency procedure for this included putting the tailhook down and engaging the approach end cable for a quick stop since, without utility hydraulic pressure, normal braking wasn't available. The aircraft did have an emergency brake accumulator that provided hydraulic pressure for up to six brake applications, depending on how hard you applied the brakes. If you couldn't get it stopped in those six or less applications, you became simply a passenger in a runaway jet. Hence the requirement to take the cable. Although a fairly serious emergency, it wasn't anything to get overly tense about.

However, when I checked the landing gear indications, the tension level rose a bit higher. The indications were that both main gear were down and locked, but the nose gear was unsafe. Apparently, the system had failed immediately after unlocking the landing gear doors and gear uplocks—the main landing gear, heavier and helped by gravity, extended to the locked position. But the nose gear, which extended forward into the airstream, was not fully extended and locked.

Still, no reason to get overly tense. The aircraft had a back-up pneumatic system charged to 3,000 psi for emergency lowering of the landing gear and flaps in the event of hydraulic failure. I activated it and checked the nose gear position indicator. Still unsafe! I then checked the pneumatic system pressure gauge, and it indicated zero pressure. With both the normal utility hydraulic system and the emergency pneumatic system at zero pressure, and the nose gear not extended, what previously had been no big deal had now become a very big deal, and the tension level rose accordingly.

I declared an emergency with the Luke control tower and informed them of the situation. They asked an airborne aircraft to join up with me and check the status of my landing gear. That pilot confirmed that the main gear were down and locked, but the nose gear was canted back about 45 degrees, unable to extend due to the force of the airstream. The folks in the control tower anticipated that if I had to crash land without a nosegear, the runway would be closed for quite a while, so they started recalling their airborne aircraft. They informed them that there was a serious emergency in progress and instructed them to return to base and land immediately.

A little later, the tower informed me that base authorities were trying to put through a conference call to the aircraft manufacturer, McDonnell Douglas in St. Louis, and get the engineers on the phone to see if they had any suggestions for getting that nosegear down and locked. By this time, the operations, maintenance, and safety folks at Luke were fully involved and were on tower radio frequency, so we had direct communication with each other. One person suggested they get a tanker airborne so I could take on fuel, which would give them more time to try and contact those engineers in St. Louis. I informed him that, since the air refueling door was operated by utility hydraulic pressure, and I had lost that system, there was no way I could air refuel. After a moment of silence, he responded, "Oh yeah, that's right, I forgot about that."

I attempted to get that nosegear fully extended by pulling positive G forces, hoping that the Gs would force that gear into the downlocks. After numerous unsuccessful attempts at this, it became obvious that bright idea wasn't going to work out. I then decided to fly a landing approach and bounce the aircraft hard on the runway with the two main landing gear, hoping that the force of that would swing the nosegear all the way forward into the downlocks. I had to be very careful not to let the nose come down, so I flew the approach at an airspeed well above normal, which gave me good stabilizer and pitch control. Also, I didn't have flaps available, since without hydraulics or pneumatics, there was no way to extend them. That too, required a higher approach speed.

I flew the approach and hit the runway hard. The chase pilot, who had previously joined up with me, stayed with me in loose formation during the attempt. He said that the nosegear swung forward, but not all the way, when I slammed the main gear on the runway. Then it returned to its 45-degree position. I tried it again, with the same unsuccessful result. There seemed to be no way to get that nosegear down and locked.

After that, I just circled the base, burning off fuel and waiting for the folks on the ground to get that conference call through to the McDonnell Douglas engineers. They didn't seem to be having much success. I must confess, however, that I wasn't in a big hurry to land. It wasn't that I was all that worried about landing the jet without a nosegear. Anxious yes, as in all emergencies, but I was confident that I could crash land the aircraft without a nosegear gently enough so the aircraft would sustain only minimal damage, as long as the two main gear remained down and locked.

And I confess there was another matter that worried me more than the impending crash landing. My main concern was the amount of time that had elapsed since we had quit drinking in the wee hours of that morning. To the best of my recollection, it was eleven hours or a little more.

Air Force regulations prohibited consuming any alcoholic beverages within twelve hours of flight. Also, as I mentioned in the account of my first crash landing, whenever a pilot is involved in an aircraft accident, which I certainly was about to be, a flight surgeon goes with the crash crew to the aircraft and immediately takes the pilot from the aircraft to the hospital. They draw seven vials of blood and check it for alcohol, drugs, medications, and anything else that could affect one's flying ability. Again, I wasn't sure what time I had had my last drink early that morning, but I suspected I was either right on the edge of that twelve-hour time window or inside it. If they found alcohol in my blood as the pilot in control, I was in big, big trouble even if I had handled that emergency perfectly. Once again, I had a vision of possibly losing my wings. So I wanted to delay landing as long as possible.

As I recall, the folks on the ground finally succeeded in getting the conference call through to McDonnell Douglas, but the company's engineers couldn't suggest anything I hadn't tried. By then, my fuel state was getting low, and it was very late in the afternoon with sunset approaching. And I certainly didn't want to land that aircraft without a nosegear in semi-darkness. I informed the tower that I would have to land shortly. They told me the emergency response crew was about to start foaming the first 3,000 ft. of the center portion of the runway with a fire retardant mixture, whereupon I would be cleared to land.

I decided to jettison the 600-gallon centerline fuel tank before landing. It was empty of fuel but full of fumes. I was concerned that when I lowered the aircraft nose all the way to the runway, the centerline tank might also impact the concrete and, in all probability, come apart. There were certainly going to be plenty of sparks and possibly flames coming from the nose sliding on concrete, and that combined with the fuel fumes could cause an explosion.

The control tower cleared me to proceed to the jettison area at the White Tanks mountains. When over the area, I pushed the emergency jettison button to blow off the tank. Nothing happened. Then I remembered that, with the main landing gear down, the jettison button was deactivated to prevent someone jettisoning tanks, bombs, or other external stores on the ramp. To reactivate it with gear down, you had to reach behind the left console and depress and hold the emergency jettison override switch while at the same time depressing the jettison button. I gave Charley control of the aircraft since I needed both hands to do that. With a thump, the centerline tank separated from the belly of the aircraft.

The runway was foamed, the fire and crash crews were in place, and I was cleared to land. I mentally reviewed a few things with Charley while setting up for the approach. First, do not deploy the drag chute immediately upon touchdown as was the normal habit pattern since that would slam the nose down so hard that structural damage to the aircraft, not to mention physical damage to Charley and myself, would certainly occur. I would pull the drag chute handle after I laid the nose down. Second, pull the emergency brake handle immediately so I would have available those six brake applications before the hydraulic pressure in the accumulator was depleted. I would need that emergency braking, not only to bring the aircraft to a stop but to keep the nose straight and avoid going outside the foamed area or off the runway for that matter, since nosegear steering was inoperative without utility hydraulics. Finally, land at a fast airspeed, so I had total pitch control of the nose. Charley and I reviewed the emergency ground egress procedures in case the aircraft caught fire.

I turned final approach and set the airspeed at 175 to 180 kts. to ensure pitch control and enable me to keep the nose up after touchdown. I touched down on the main gear and started to lower the nose slowly, slowly, to the foamed concrete. I remember being surprised at how far the nose went down before it contacted the runway. It seemed that every time I expected it to touch down, it kept going down further. If it hadn't been for the locked shoulder harness, I would have fallen forward in the seat.

I did manage to lay the nose down very smoothly, but at the speed we were traveling, when metal met concrete, it was still quite a jolt. I remember feeling a momentary, sharp pain at the base of my spine when the nose contacted the runway. In spite of the foam, the sound of the aircraft nose sliding on that concrete runway was terrible.

Immediately after the nose contacted the runway, I deployed the drag chute and pulled the emergency brake handle. I applied gradual pressure to the brakes to avoid using up those six applications too quickly, and also used the brakes to keep the aircraft's nose pointed straight down the runway centerline and into the foam whenever the friction started to pull it to the side. With the combination of the drag chute, the emergency brakes, and the friction of aircraft metal sliding on concrete, the aircraft came to a stop within a couple thousand feet or so. The crash crews were there immediately and started shooting foam on the hot nose section to prevent fire. When

Charley and I opened our canopies, we got a stream of foam in the cockpits. I frantically signaled for them to cease and desist, which they did.

As I unstrapped to leave the cockpit, I noticed on my left a hand reaching in towards me. It was the Commanding General of Luke AFB, who said that he wanted to shake my hand and congratulate me on a superb act of flying. Charley and I exited the aircraft, and the Chief of Flying Safety for Luke AFB, whom I had known when he was stationed at George AFB, said he would give us a ride to his office where we could start writing our depositions. The accident investigators would need all the details of the emergency and crash landing. To my surprise, there was no flight surgeon in sight to take us to the hospital for those blood samples, which was very unusual. I didn't say anything since I was still very worried about whether my blood would show alcohol content.

When we got to the Flight Safety Office, my friend asked if we would like a beer. We both said, "You bet!" He had a fridge in his office with some cold beer. As soon as I opened that can of beer and took the first swallow, I knew I was home free and could quit worrying.

And sure enough, shortly afterward, the phone rang. It was the Base Hospital, asking if that pilot who just crash-landed the F-4 was there. When my friend told them yes and that I was writing up my deposition, he was told, "Well, get him to the hospital immediately so we can take blood." They were also very surprised to hear that there had not been a flight surgeon at the scene. When we arrived at the hospital, I told them I had just had a beer in the safety office. I apologized for messing up their blood test and said, "I'm sure you can understand that a cold beer was sure inviting after the stress and excitement of the emergency." They agreed but said they had to take blood anyway. And so, they drew seven vials of my blood.

The next morning, out of curiosity, I checked with them to see how the samples had come out. They told me that since I had that beer, the samples were invalid, and they trashed them. I gave silent thanks that my friend had that beer in his office.

The news of our crash landing made the rounds of the squadrons. That night, the bar at the Officers' Club was crowded with flyers, and I couldn't buy a drink. The F-104 squadron commander bought me a drink and said I could fly in his squadron anytime. One of the F-4 squadron commanders invited us to brief his pilots and weapon systems officers the next morning on the emergency and how we had handled it. We agreed to do so.

As I recall, I had at least four martinis that night and didn't pay for a one. I'm not sure what Charley had. And I remember clearly that I didn't feel any effect whatsoever from those drinks. Zip, zero, not even a buzz. It was if I had been drinking water. The only reason I can think of is that my adrenalin level was still so high it neutralized the effects of alcohol. Not being a medical type, I don't know if that is even possible. But I do know this. I left the Officers' Club and walked a perfectly straight line to the Officers' Quarters where I went to bed and slept like a baby. The next morning, after Charley and I briefed those F-4 pilots and WSOs, as we were invited to do, we caught a ride home with a couple of pilots who were driving to George AFB.

The investigators found the reason for our losing both the utility hydraulic system and the pneumatic system. There was a crack in the nosegear cylinder that dumped the hydraulic fluid and air pressure overboard before the nosegear could reach the down and locked position. The official finding for the accident was a material failure. Also, as it turned out, the only damage to the aircraft as a result of the landing was that the bottom of the nose and radome was scraped up a bit. Within two days, maintenance had that fixed and the nosegear cylinder replaced and the aircraft was flying again.

Some months later, while I was attending Armed Forces Staff College in Virginia, my seminar instructor called me to the front of the class and presented me with the Tactical Air Command Pilot of

Distinction Award for recovering that aircraft from a serious emergency with minimal damage. Charley, who I believe was still at George AFB at the time, also got one.

I sometimes think of how differently it could have turned out if my friend the Safety Officer had not offered me that beer.

CHAPTER 23

STAFF TOUR: ITALY

After graduation from Armed Forces Staff College in Norfolk, Virginia, in January 1977, I was assigned to NATO Headquarters, Southern Europe in Naples, Italy, as a tactical air operations officer. The Command's area of responsibility stretched from Spain to the Middle East, encompassing the entire Mediterranean region, and was composed of Army, Navy, and Air Force components of the United States, Italy, Turkey, and Greece. The Commander-in-Chief was a four-star U.S. Navy Admiral, and the Air Force component was commanded by a three-star general, who was our boss. Our operations branch, like the other branches in the headquarters, had officers and enlisted personnel from all the countries represented.

Although this was a non-flying staff tour, and this memoir is mainly limited to flying experiences, I include it because even though I initially tried to get out of the assignment, and my wife was not at all enthused over it, in retrospect, it was our best assignment from a family standpoint. It was also a turning point in my life when I realized that if I was going to claim to be a Christian, I had better get serious about my faith as I had been in my younger years, and both grow in that faith and live it. Thanks to God, my wife, and an officer in the operations branch with whom I had been previously stationed in Germany, I did that.

Living in southern Italy was a culture shock for many of the Americans, especially the wives, but most adjusted quickly and came to enjoy it immensely. Louise and I loved it. We rented a two-story villa with an entire rooftop patio overlooking the Tyrrhenian Sea in a beautiful hilly area covered with villas, trees, and flowers. It was called Parco Azzurro and located a short distance north of Naples on the road to Rome. It was home to many Italian as well as American families. We had an exceptionally tight-knit chapel group, as well as close friendships with others in our Parco and other housing areas. Many of the friendships we made in Italy have lasted through the years to the present day.

And then there was the food—ah, the food! We can truthfully say, and often do say, that in three and a half years in Italy, we never had a bad or even a mediocre meal. Eating out in restaurants and family cafes in Italy was a different experience. It was an evening's entertainment, the high point of the day where you took your time savoring the various courses and then taking a break between them to enjoy the strong red wine and the companionship and conversation of friends. A two- or three-hour meal was not uncommon. There was no hurry, no attempt to get customers in and out, and the local custom seemed to be that the table you were sitting at was yours for the evening. To this day, Italian food is my favorite, although normally it is not quite the same in America as in Italy.

The driving experience in Naples is impossible to describe in words. The most dangerous drivers in Naples and the surrounding area were the Americans and other foreigners who had just arrived and who were still under the quaint impression that traffic rules, speed limits, stop signs, and traffic lights were to be obeyed. It didn't take long for us to learn that the purpose of traffic lights was to burn electricity and the purpose of traffic rules and speed limits was to fix blame in the event of an accident. Otherwise, they were to be ignored. When you approached a red light or stop sign, you simply went through it if you could beat the other car coming in the other direction. And if it was going to be close, the trick was not to let the other driver know you saw him. If he was unsure whether or not you saw him, he would probably slow down and give you the right of way, and you would win the contest. But if you looked in his direction, and he knew you saw him, you better give him the right of way because he wasn't going to stop. If being a law-abiding American, you stopped at that light or stop sign when you had room to beat the oncoming traffic, you would have the drivers behind you laying on their horns and probably saying to themselves, "dumb American."

Another common Italian driving procedure was that if all lanes going in your direction were filled with traffic, and you were in a hurry, you simply pulled into one of the lanes supposedly reserved for traffic going in the opposite direction and used it. And if all lanes in both directions were filled and a sidewalk was available, you drove on the sidewalk. Remember, we are talking about small cars. My wife had an interesting experience one night when she was driving to the chapel on the Navy base. The soccer game had just let out, and the traffic leaving the stadium was bumper to bumper. Traffic jams in Naples were monumental, like nothing I had ever seen before or since. Anyway, not only were the lanes leaving the stadium jammed, but also the lanes going toward the stadium, the direction in which my wife was going, were jammed with traffic going in the wrong direction—in other words, heading towards her. Since we had been in Italy for a couple of years and had developed driving habits similar to the Italians, this didn't surprise or faze my wife. She simply pulled off the road onto the sidewalk and continued on her way.

Then she was met by another car driving on the sidewalk in the opposite direction. The two stopped, facing each other. The other driver, a man and seeing that a woman drove the car facing him, brusquely waved his arms motioning for my wife to pull to the side and let him pass. Louise shook her head "No!" As I said, we had by then become quite adept at driving Italian style. The Italian waved his arms even more wildly, indicating that Louise should get out of his way. Louise then turned off the ignition, sat back with her arms folded across her chest, and again shook her head "No!" After a little more arm-waving, the man finally realized he had met his match and moved his car to the side so Louise could pass. She then continued driving down the sidewalk until the soccer stadium traffic had passed and she was able to get back on the road. I told her later that, given the Italian male's macho attitude and personality, she had probably caused extensive psychological damage to the man. He'd had his family in the car with him, and he had lost face in front of them, and to a woman no less.

Many of the American wives wouldn't drive in Naples unless they absolutely had to. The vast majority of men, including myself, thoroughly enjoyed it. Where else can you bend the rules, if not throw them out altogether, and push the limits when driving? Fighter pilots enjoyed driving in Naples. Now, given all the above, you may think that the accident rate was off the charts. Accidents, however, were rare. In three and a half years, I think I saw less than a half dozen accidents. Italian drivers may have been crazy, but they were very good at handling a car.

When living in Italy, one is literally surrounded by history, priceless art, cathedrals, museums, and Roman ruins. Just to the north of where we lived, on the highway to Rome, was the main aqueduct, which in the days of the Roman Empire carried the water supply to Rome. Just behind the area where our villa was located was the cobble-stoned Appian Way, the ancient road from southern Italy to Rome. The headquarters where I worked was a twenty-minute drive from our villa and was in itself a drive through history.

As I would leave our villa and approach a curve in the road, there just across the way were the arch and the ruins of Cuma, the oldest Greek settlement in Italy, dating from the early B.C. period. As I drove a little further, I passed Lake Averno, beautiful and yet foreboding, the bottom of which, as legend has it, is the entrance to hell. Just past the lake is the charming seaport village of Puzzuoli, which in the Book of Acts of the Bible is named Puteli, where the ship carrying the Apostle Paul from Israel put into port when he was taken to Rome to appear before Caesar. A short distance further, I passed Sulfatari on my left, an active volcano that frequently sent steam clouds into the air with its accompanying heavy sulfur odor. And then, also on my left, I would pass the ruins of a large coliseum, the second or third best-preserved coliseum in Italy. Needless to say, I have never had a drive to work that came anywhere near being as fascinating as my drive to work in Italy.

The key to enjoying living in southern Italy, as my wife and I and our friends discovered, is to appreciate the attitude and lifestyle of the people, which basically is, "if it doesn't get done today, there is always tomorrow"— or *domani*, as the Italians say. So don't sweat it! Americans, given our work ethic, found this attitude somewhat difficult to get used to. For example, it was not uncommon at NATO headquarters for the American personnel to still be at their desks long after the other foreign military personnel had left. Nevertheless, to a great degree, we did adopt the local attitude that one must enjoy life, be thankful for it, and not be dominated by schedules or become overly frustrated, anxious, or flustered over the small stuff. Enjoying the good life in Italy consisted mainly of good food, good wine, good company, and beautiful scenery.

Even our son and daughter, who were nine and five years old when we arrived, and twelve and eight years old when we left, have good memories of Italy. And my wife? Well, she cried and cried when we left. Of all the places we have lived or been to during our military career, whether overseas or in the States, her favorite memories are of Italy.

And by the way, the rent for our large villa overlooking the sea and surrounded by trees and flowers, which I previously mentioned, was three hundred dollars a month.

CHAPTER 24

FLIGHT TO CAIRO, EGYPT (F-4E)

After my staff tour in Italy and another short tour at George AFB, California, I was assigned to the 406th Tactical Fighter Training Wing at Zaragoza AB, Spain, as Assistant Deputy Commander of Operations. One day, we received a tasking from higher headquarters to pick up an F-4E at Torrejon AB in Madrid, perform a local check flight to ensure all systems were operational, and then deliver it to the Egyptian Air Force at a base near Cairo. Since I had never been to Egypt, and this was too good an opportunity to pass up, I asked my boss if he had any objections to my taking the jet to Cairo, along with Tommy Graves, the weapon systems officer who worked for us. I was told to go for it.

Tom and I hitched a ride to Torrejon AB, flew the jet on a local checkout flight that day, and found it to be Code One—that is, all systems go. We would depart for Cairo the next morning and be accompanied by an F-16. Once over Egypt, the F-16 pilot would break away and head to another base where he would turn the jet over to the Egyptians. We would continue on to Cairo. We received an extensive briefing from the command's foreign military aircraft delivery personnel. It included the route, the traffic control agencies along the route, navigation aids in Egypt (which were sparse and had a reputation for being unreliable), the layout of the Egyptian air base where we would be landing, and some local customs and cultural characteristics they thought we should be aware of.

We would rendezvous with a KC-135 tanker crew over the Mediterranean Sea, which would provide us air refueling support until we approached the coast of Egypt, at which time he would break away and return to his home base. After the briefing, we went to the Officers' Club for dinner, then to the Officers' Quarters for a good night's sleep before the long flight the next day.

The takeoff and tanker rendezvous went well, and the F-16 pilot and I each took up a loose formation position on opposite sides of the tanker and settled in for the flight. As I recall, it was to last for five hours or more and consisted of four air refuelings. The flight across the Mediterranean brought back memories of Chuck's and my flight to Tehran.

I have previously mentioned how the cockpit of a jet fighter can get very uncomfortable after a few hours. Restrained by the parachute harness, lap belt, survival kit connections, leg restraints, and so on, the ability to stretch and exercise arms and legs is severely limited. In addition, you are sitting on a survival kit with a firm surface because having a soft cushion between your butt and the ejection seat would result in severe spinal injury if you had to eject. All in all, after some hours, the extremities become cramped, and the butt starts to ache or go numb. But, hey, that's a small price to pay for being one of the privileged few whose office is the cockpit of a modern jet fighter.

The flight was quite enjoyable. It was a beautiful day, with visibility unlimited, giving us a clear view of Sicily, Athens, and Crete as we made our way eastward. Finally, with the coastline of Egypt in sight, the tanker turned back, and after we made landfall, the F-16 pilot turned toward his destination, and we took up a heading for Cairo West airbase.

The landmass was all brown and as flat as a billiard table, with no landmarks or geographic features to use to fix our position. However, I knew that on an easterly heading, we would reach the Nile Delta, the fertile, green area on the banks of the Nile River. Using the Delta as a reference, it would be easy to locate the airbase.

As we descended from altitude and proceeded east, the visibility started to get worse. And then suddenly, we were amid a raging sandstorm with visibility virtually zero. I had Tom tune in the ground navigation facility located near the base, hoping to get a good fix on its location. No luck! The bearing pointer rotated around the instrument's face and didn't receive a signal it could lock onto. Apparently, the facility was inoperative, which didn't come as a big surprise to me, given the briefing we had received on the status of local flight facilities and equipment. I tried to communicate with local air traffic control, also with no success.

Tom and I searched intensely for the Nile River Delta's green, fertile band in the otherwise featureless, brown desert landscape. But the sandstorm was so thick I could barely see the nose of the aircraft, much less anything on the ground. Our fuel status was also starting to get somewhat low. The thought crossed my mind that having to eject over the barren desert in the midst of a sandstorm would certainly be an ignominious end to the mission. We would have delivered the aircraft to Egypt, but not in the way intended.

Then the intensity of the sandstorm decreased and suddenly stopped altogether. And lo and behold, the bearing pointer on the navigation system locked onto the ground signal and gave us a bearing to the airbase. And with visibility restored, we soon saw the green Nile Delta and the airbase west of Cairo.

One of the American F-4 instructor pilots, assigned there to instruct Egyptian pilots in the aircraft, was in the tower to give us instructions. The first instruction he gave us was to disregard the long, smooth asphalt runway that was clearly visible. He said that it was a fake runway to deceive Israeli or other enemy pilots. The real runway was a concrete strip just to the west of it. Upon landing, I noticed that the runway had cracks in it and weeds growing through the cracks, and it appeared as if it had not been cleaned or swept for weeks. Turning off the runway, the appearance of the taxiway was even worse. Stones, rocks, and other foreign debris were clearly visible. I was sure we would suck some of that debris into the engine intakes before we reached the parking area, but fortunately, we didn't. The instructor pilot told us later that the condition of the runway and taxiway was normal, and he was constantly amazed that they hadn't yet damaged or ruined any engines because of foreign object ingestion.

However, their condition, as bad as it was, was good compared to the rest of the base. To say it was austere would be a monumental understatement. The buildings, mud adobe structures, were shabby and in an advanced state of disrepair, with apparently little or no maintenance and no concern for appearance. While taxiing in, we noticed an old weather-beaten Russian Badger bomber that showed serious signs of deterioration. Also, I was surprised to see bombs and missiles, including modern electro-optical guided missiles, stacked out in the open unprotected from the elements. I had been to a lot of airbases in various parts of the world, including some third-world nations, but had never seen anything like this. I had to agree with the American instructor pilot who said that if any American pilot complained about their base facilities in the States, they should be sent to Cairo West for a tour of duty.

To top it off, there were dogs all over the place. When I asked the American pilot about all the dogs, he said they were strays, looking for scraps of food. He told a story about some Chinese personnel who had been there for training some months past. The Chinese asked if the dogs had owners. When informed that they were strays, their response was, "You mean no one owns them?"

191

The American pilot said that, shortly afterward, the dog population noticeably decreased; dog apparently was a delicacy for the Chinese.

Tom and I packed our luggage in a van, and the instructor took us into Cairo to the hotel where he and the rest of the American contingent were staying. We were amazed! It was a huge five-star resort with all the amenities, including a huge, fancy pool, a first-class restaurant, and beautiful landscaping. And best of all, it was situated within a short walking distance to the Sphinx and the Pyramids of Giza. The American instructors had one-half of the entire third floor, and we received a room in their area. I had stayed in some fancy places in Europe and Asia, but this was the top of the top of the line.

The next morning after breakfast, Tom and I took the walk to the Sphinx and the Pyramids. We noticed that there were horse stables in the area and that you could rent horses and explore the area and the pyramids some distance from the main pyramid on horseback. We did this and had a great time riding those horses from one pyramid to the next. We discovered an empty sarcophagus in the desert sand, so I stretched out inside of it, crossed my hands over my chest, and had Tom take a picture. It was a memorable day for both of us, and we appreciated the fact that, as military flyers, we had the opportunity to see much of the world, visit exotic places, and enjoy many unique experiences, such as horseback riding around the Pyramids of Giza.

Over the next couple of days, we hired a car and driver, who also functioned as a guide to show us Cairo and the surrounding area. If I had to describe Cairo in one word, it would be "chaos." The traffic was horrendous, with everything from new Mercedes to 1950s-vintage automobiles to horse-and donkey-drawn carts to loud motor scooters with their exhaust stench. Our driver was the speedy type and expertly maneuvered his way through the maze of traffic. He took us to many places over the next several days, from downtown

Cairo to other historical and archaeological sites some distance from the city.

Our guide took us to the site containing some step pyramids, which were different from the smooth-sided ones at Giza. We went inside the largest pyramid and descended through the corridor leading to the burial chamber. We viewed the wall paintings and hieroglyphics, which were in surprisingly good condition given they were thousands of years old. He also took us to a site that contained the ruins of hundreds of stables, where the Pharaoh or some other high official had kept his horses and chariots. We drove along the Nile River to view some of the villages and settlements along the waterway.

In Cairo, we visited the famous Cairo Museum, which was huge and very impressive. Although we spent a good part of the day there, it wasn't even a minuscule fraction of the time required to explore the place. Nevertheless, we were fascinated by the mummies, the priceless treasures taken from various tombs, and the vast number of other rare and priceless relics and artifacts.

Our driver also took us to the bazaar in downtown Cairo. It extended for blocks and was even more exotic than the one Chuck and I had seen in Tehran. The air was pungent with the smell of spices and an unending variety of foods, and we were surrounded by the noise of the crowds dealing, bargaining, and arguing with the vendors, and the cries of those vendors selling their wares. They included just about anything you could think of, from jewelry to gold and brass and bronze, furniture, rugs and kitchenware, clothing and shoes, perfumes and silk, and on and on. Altogether, the sights, sounds, and smells were unique, to say the least.

While at the bazaar, a young Egyptian man approached Tom and me and asked if we were Americans. When we answered yes, he said, "You are very welcome in our country." This was in 1984. I wonder what his response would be today, since America, although envied by virtually all nations, is disliked by many of those nations and downright hated by the majority of Muslim nations. In my opinion, this reflects both irony and appalling ingratitude, since it was primarily the United States that freed Kuwait from Saddam Hussein's brutality, conquest, and bloody tyranny during the Gulf War of 1991. It was primarily the United States that saved Saudi Arabia from the same fate. It was primarily the United States that stepped in to save the Muslims of Kosovo from the genocide conducted by the Serbs when the European nations refused to take action to stop the genocide taking place in their own backyard. It was primarily the United States that freed the Iraqi people from one of the most evil, bloody, and cruel dictators in modern history—that same Saddam Hussein. It was primarily the United States that rendered huge amounts of humanitarian aid and assistance to Muslim countries devastated by tsunamis, earthquakes, and other natural disasters. Never in the history of nations has there been a nation as benevolent and generous as the United States, and much of this benevolence and generosity has been bestowed on Muslim peoples. One can be forgiven for asking, "Where's the gratitude?"

And as far as Western Europe is concerned, had it not been for the United States coming to their assistance and pulling their irons out of the fire with our blood and treasure during two World Wars, not to mention the exorbitant cost of providing an umbrella of defense for them from Communist aggression for over forty years, they would all be under the heel of either Nazism or Communism today. And yet, most of those nations, which take pride in their so-called sophistication, never pass up a chance to insult or condemn America and its leaders. Ingratitude is the mark of the ignorant and the hypocrite.

When I wonder how many people around the world today would say to Americans, as that Egyptian did back in 1984, "You are very welcome in our country," I can only answer, "Probably not many."

I asked our driver to take Tom and me to the place where Anwar Sadat was assassinated. He said it was restricted to visitors;

nevertheless, he would take us there, but we couldn't get out of the car. As we approached the location, he had us bend over in our seats so no one outside could see us. He parked in front of the stands where the assassination had taken place, and when all was clear, told us we could sit up. He showed us where Sadat had been sitting and how the assassins had been able to approach him and kill him. We could tell that the driver was getting uncomfortable and afraid we would be seen, and so we left.

On the way back, the driver took a sandwich out of a bag and started eating it. This was during Ramadan. I told him I thought all Muslims fasted until evening during Ramadan. He gave me a weak smile, shrugged his shoulders, and continued eating. We crossed a bridge over the Nile River, and he took us to the outskirts of the city and showed us a refugee town. I distinctly remember the scene as one of absolute squalor and grinding poverty and wondered why the authorities didn't do something to alleviate those peoples' terrible conditions. Returning to our five-star resort hotel after that scene was an utter, absolute contrast of extreme opposites. When we arrived at the hotel, we settled with the driver and were generous paying him. He had been an outstanding guide, both informative and friendly.

We spent our last day in Cairo checking out the Sphinx and the Pyramids again, lounged around the pool, and enjoyed an excellent dinner at the hotel's first-class restaurant. We then packed up for departure. The next morning, we caught a flight from Cairo to Madrid, and then a local flight to Zaragoza. Another adventure in the life of a military aviator had come to an end.

CHAPTER 25

MID-AIR COLLISION WITH A TURKEY BUZZARD (F-4E)

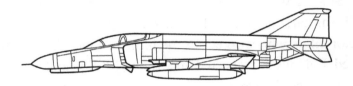

Z aragoza Air Base, Spain, was the premier weapons training base for the American fighter squadrons in Europe. The squadrons deployed from their home bases in Germany and England to Zaragoza, Spain, on the average of twice a year for a couple of weeks or more so the aviators could update their semi-annual currency in dive-bombing, strafing, simulated nuclear weapons delivery, and air-to-air tactics and gunnery. Although training facilities for this purpose were available in Germany and England, the normal lousy weather and heavily populated areas around these facilities often restricted or precluded such training. The great advantage of Zaragoza was its wide-open spaces and normally excellent flying weather. As the Assistant Director of Operations (ADO) and instructor pilot, it was my privilege to fly with these squadrons, and especially with the deployed F-4 squadrons.

The weapons training facility at Zaragoza, used for training both American and Spanish fighter pilots, was the Bardenas Reales Bombing and Gunnery Range, located some thirty miles from Zaragoza Air Base. It was, without a doubt, the busiest weapons range in all of Europe, and at that time, it would not be an exaggeration to say the busiest in the world. Our Operations Division also had the responsibility of assisting the Spanish in the maintenance and upkeep of this extensive and vitally important training facility.

Fighter pilots have a reputation for flying hard and playing hard—a reputation certainly exhibited during their many deployments. As ADO, I was the one in the command chain who flew most often with the deployed F-4 squadrons and socialized with them. Since I was considerably older than the majority of these pilots, I was naturally pleased when, one day, the local F-4 weapons instructor pilots who worked for me informed me privately that the deployed F-4 pilots respected my flying ability and were of the opinion that I could handle the jet with the best of them. Also, they said that the deployed WSOs all liked to fly with me since it was not unusual for me to win the bets on bombing and strafing scores made before each mission, and they naturally got to share in the winnings.

The rapport I had with these deployed aviators led to a situation where they considered me as sort of a buffer between them and the top base authorities when their playing got too hard and out of hand. I won't go into the many occasions when I received a call late at night to come to the Officers' Club or BOQ to handle a situation that was getting out of hand. I'll mention only one occurrence I think the reader will enjoy. I thought I had seen or experienced just about everything fighter pilots could come up with, but this one took even me by surprise.

It occurred late on a Friday evening after a week of heavy flying, and the flyers were unwinding at the Officers' Club bar. The bar was about to close, and it was raining heavily outside. Maria, one of the Spanish barmaids, happened to mention that she was going to get soaking wet going to her car in the parking lot. Maria had worked at the Club for a long time, and she was both familiar and patient with the unruly ways of a bunch of fighter pilots. She was well known and well-liked by all the aviators who treated her courteously and tipped her generously.

Two of the pilots, who had been drinking for some time and feeling no pain, decided that they were not going to let Maria get soaked by the rain. They went to the parking lot and located her car, which was a small Spanish automobile about the size of a Volkswagen bug. They put the car in neutral and proceeded to push it to the Officers' Club entrance. But instead of leaving it there, they enlisted the help of their buddies who held the double doors of the Club open while they pushed that car inside and parked it in the Officers' Club lobby. They then went to the bar and escorted Maria to her car. She was dumbfounded to find her car in the lobby of the Officers' Club.

When I was informed of this escapade the next morning, my first reaction was to laugh. I not only thought it humorous but as a fighter pilot who had pulled a few shenanigans myself over the years, I had to admire the innovation and cavalier attitude of those two pilots. Shortly afterward, however, I received a summons to the office of the Combat Support Group Commander, who was responsible for the maintenance and upkeep of all base facilities, including the Officers' Club. When I stepped into his office, it was immediately apparent he did not see any humor whatsoever in the action of those two pilots.

The situation was made all the worse by the fact that he had just recently had new carpet installed throughout the Officers' Club. A dripping wet car with its muddy tires parked in the lobby of the Club on that new carpet nearly sent him into apoplexy. His immediate impulse was to charge those two pilots with damaging government property and send them home. He also wanted me to write a strong letter to their commander, demanding that he take disciplinary action against them.

I had to do a lot of smooth talking to get those two pilots off the hook. I personally assured the Combat Support Group Commander that those pilots would pay for any damages to the Club and the carpet. This, by the way, was the standard operating procedure, and all the deployed aviators understood and agreed that they would pay for any damages they had incurred to base facilities before deploying back to home base. I also informed the commander, in a subtle way, of the possible ramifications of sending those pilots home before they had completed their semi-annual weapons training. That could result in their losing their combat-ready status, which in turn would have an adverse impact on their squadron's combat readiness rating. This would cause major concern at USAFE headquarters level, as well as at the Pentagon, and we, in turn, could be criticized for not allowing them to complete their training. He eventually calmed down and agreed to let them stay and finish their training on the condition that I give them a strong reprimand and they pay for repairing and cleaning the Officers' Club carpet. This was done. I had trouble keeping from laughing when I gave them what passed as a reprimand, and they knew it. I also told them to cool it and behave like a couple of choirboys during the remainder of their deployment. The sequel to this episode was that, after a short time, the Combat Support Group Commander's temper cooled, and he even acknowledged the humor and uniqueness associated with that cavalier action of those pilots.

The turkey buzzard incident, which is the main theme of this section, occurred during an air-to-ground range mission. The Spanish had astutely (and I use the term facetiously) located a bird sanctuary close to the Bardenas Reales Bombing and Gunnery Range. They would place animal carcasses there for the birds to feed on. These weren't your garden variety birds. They were large condors, buzzards, vultures, and so forth, some with wingspans up to six feet. There had been bird strikes on the range over the years, and as I recall, at least two pilots had been killed when impacting one of these large birds at high speed.

On this particular mission, our weapons events were dive-bombing, strafing, and simulated nuclear weapons deliveries. The visibility on the range was often a little hazy due to the Spanish burning off their fields in the surrounding area. Because of this, I often flew on the range with my helmet visor up to have a clearer view of the target, regardless of the potential for bird strikes at the low altitudes at which we flew for weapons delivery. This, undoubtedly, also reflected the fighter pilot's attitude that "it can happen to the other guy, but not to me." However, for some reason, I had my helmet visor down that day, covering my face and eyes. I don't know why, since it was an exception to my habit pattern, but thank God it was so.

I rolled in for a low altitude nuclear weapons delivery to drop a Mk-106 practice bomb that had the ballistics and trajectory of a nuclear bomb. I descended to 200 ft. above the ground, pushed the power up, and increased speed to 540 kts. (close to 600 mph). As I approached the bomb release point, I checked the radar altimeter to ensure I was at 200 ft. altitude with the airspeed indicator for 540 kts.

Just prior to the sight aiming point reaching the target, there was a loud explosion, the cockpit filled with condensation, and I felt something impact both my right shoulder and my helmet visor and oxygen mask. I lost all visibility and couldn't see anything. Since I was very low to the ground and at a very high airspeed, instinct took over. I pulled the control stick back and kept it centered, shoved the throttles forward, and climbed for altitude. While climbing, and after we were out of danger of impacting the ground, I raised my visor so I could see. It was immediately apparent what had happened.

There was a huge gaping hole in the right side of the cockpit windscreen, with nearly all of the thick Plexiglas missing. The cockpit and my flight suit were spattered with the remains of what obviously had been a very large bird. I gave control of the aircraft momentarily to my WSO so I could take off my helmet and check the visor. It wasn't broken, but it was covered with dried blood and bird remains. That explained the impact I had felt on my visor and oxygen mask and my loss of visibility. The impact to my right shoulder was caused by a large piece of that three-fourth inch thick Plexiglas, designed to withstand small arms fire but apparently not the impact of a large bird at 600 mph. I found out later that pieces of that windscreen had gone down the intake of the right engine and caused engine damage; nevertheless, the engine had continued operating with all indications normal.

I took back control of the aircraft from my WSO, slowed down to an airspeed of 250 kts., and gave a Mayday (emergency) call on the radio, informing both the range control officer and the control tower personnel at Zaragoza of what had happened. One of the other aircraft in our flight joined up to escort us back to base and checked our aircraft over for any signs of additional damage that might affect landing. He could see none. With the large gaping hole in the right side of the windscreen, I had to fly the aircraft leaning way over to the left to be free of the windblast at 250 kts. Approaching the base, I flew a straight-in final approach and landed with no problem.

The cockpit was a mess, and I apologized to the crew chief for bringing his aircraft back in that condition since he would have to remove the ejection seat and clean the cockpit of all bird remains. Then I was taken to our flight surgeon, Capt. Charles Johnson, who checked me over after I got out of my stinking flight suit. He pulled a few small pieces of what he thought were bird residue from my right shoulder with tweezers, gave me a tetanus shot, and pronounced me fit for duty. The bird residue in the cockpit was later determined to be that of a turkey buzzard.

I called Base Supply and told them to get a new flight suit to me at the hospital right away. I was sure no amount of washing would completely remove the stink of those bird remains from the fabric. Besides, I had no desire to wear that flight suit again.

Over the years, I often wondered about that impulse that caused me to lower my visor that day when, as I mentioned, it was my habit pattern to leave it up on days of hazy visibility. After all, bombing and strafing scores were more important than taking precautions against the extremely rare possibility of the aircraft and a turkey buzzard being in the same piece of sky at the same time. And yeah, I know—that's dumb! But throughout this memoir, I have never claimed to have the market on smarts. Nevertheless, I have to admit that I was smart enough to learn from that encounter. From that time on, I flew on the range with my visor down.

It's certainly true that if I had not had the visor down that day, I would probably have ended up blind or dead. And so, I'll say again what I've said before: "The Good Lord watches out for fools and fighter pilots."

CHAPTER 26

A YOUNG LADY'S LESSON TO THIS FIGHTER PILOT

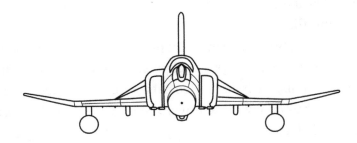

W e learn many lessons in this life—hopefully for the good. Unfortunately, we have to relearn some of those lessons due to our tendency to forget. Years ago, I relearned a lesson, and it was brought home to me from an unlikely source—a young lady. Let me tell you how it happened.

Periodically, the fighter squadrons would devote a day's flying schedule to giving incentive flights. Incentive flights were flights given to non-flying personnel for morale purposes. Crew chiefs usually had priority, since it was a big deal for them to get a flight in the jet they were assigned to maintain. However, other personnel who worked in various agencies on the base such as administration, civil engineering, finance, legal, etc., who were outstanding performers in their specialty, were recommended by their supervisors to the squadron for an incentive flight.

We fighter pilots did not especially enjoy giving incentive flights. Why? Because it was almost certain the person would get scared or sick or both, and we would have to cease doing any hard maneuvering with high G forces and spend much of the flight droning along straight and level. Our attitude was that, since they were getting a flight in a supersonic, multi-million dollar, front-line jet fighter, they should, to some extent, experience what that war machine could do. If they wanted to just fly around looking at the countryside, they could do that in a little Cessna or similar light aircraft. It wasn't that we were trying to scare them or make them sick. Far from that, we just wanted them to have an experience they would probably never have again.

It could be a bit intimidating for them getting suited up in a flight suit, a G suit, flight boots, parachute harness, helmet, oxygen mask, etc., then getting briefed on ejection procedures, being strapped into an ejection seat and a cramped cockpit surrounded by a multitude of instruments, dials, switches, rheostats, circuit breakers, etc., and finally have the canopy closed over them. One sometimes got the impression that they were thinking, "Why did I ever agree to do this?" We pilots always made sure our passengers had a few barf bags with them. We didn't want them to upchuck in the cockpit since the crew chief would have to clean it up.

On this particular day, I and my fellow pilots were scheduled to give two incentive flights each. As I went to the operations counter to meet my first victim (oops, I mean passenger), I felt encouraged. He was a young Arnold Schwarzenegger, obviously a weightlifter, who appeared as if he could walk through a brick wall. I figured I could really do lots of aerobatics and hard maneuvering with this guy. I was wrong. I'll spare you the details and just say that after the maximum performance climb after the takeoff and a few high G maneuvers, it was clear he was not enjoying the experience. We droned along until fuel got down to landing weight and landed shortly afterwards. As I recall, he said that he was glad he had the experience, but he never wanted to do that again. Also, he had filled two—or was it three?—barf bags during the flight.

As I went to the operations counter to meet my second victim (oops, I mean passenger), my heart sank. There, standing before me, was this very attractive little wisp of a gal. I doubt if she weighed a hundred pounds soaking wet. I was surprised they found flight gear small enough to fit her. I figured this would be another short flight since I couldn't imagine being able to do much in the way of aerobatics or hard maneuvering with her in the jet. I briefed her on what we would do, told her that if she got scared or started to feel sick, she should tell me immediately, and I would cease any maneuvering until she felt better.

I got her strapped into the rear cockpit and chuckled to myself as I had to raise the ejection seat as high as it would go so she could see over the canopy rails. After I got all strapped in and got electrical power on the jet, I asked her if she was okay and how she felt. I got a cheery reply: "I'm fine and feel great." As we took the runway for takeoff, I again told her not to get scared during the maximum performance climb and that I had everything under control. With that, I released brakes and advanced the throttles to afterburner.

After we were airborne, I raised the gear and flaps and held the jet low to the ground until the end of the runway, at which time we were well over 400 mph. I then pulled the jet nearly vertical, and with afterburners roaring, we climbed heavenward like a homesick angel. At twenty thousand feet, which we reached in less than a minute, I rolled the jet inverted, pulled the nose to the horizon, and did a snap aileron roll to straight and level. I asked the young lady if she was okay, and for an answer, I got a squeal of delight and "Oh, that was fantastic. I never expected anything like that—I loved it." *Well,* I thought, *so far, so good.*

I told her I was going to pull some G forces so she could experience what that felt like and if she started to feel sick to let me know. I wanted to start easy on the young lady, so I rolled the jet into a 4-G turn. I held the turn for a while, then rolled out and asked her if she felt okay. Her response? "Oh, that felt good. Do it again." Well, okay. Let's try 5 Gs. Same response. Six Gs. Same response. Seven Gs. Same response. The pressure exerted on the body at 7 Gs is seven times one's body weight, but it didn't faze her at all. I quickly realized this young lady was someone unique. I lit the afterburners and accelerated to supersonic speed so she could say she had traveled faster than the speed of sound. I then told her I would show her the jet's rapid rate of roll, and I warned her not to let the side-force Gs bang her head against the canopy. With that, I flung the control stick to the side and did two 360-degree sequential rolls in less than two seconds. I asked her if she was feeling disoriented or nauseous. "Oh, no, that was great!" she replied.

I asked her if she would like to do some aerobatics. "Oh, yes, I'd like that." I accelerated to 500 knots, pulled back on the stick, and established a 5-G pull to the vertical, easing off the Gs as we came over the top inverted at 250 knots—then with the nose pointed straight down, increased back to 5 Gs as we recovered from the dive to straight and level flight at 500 knots. Again, I heard, "That was fantastic, I loved it, do more." I gave her control of the jet and had her do a couple of aileron rolls. She liked that.

Needless to say, I was enjoying myself along with her. Given the mission profiles we flew, it wasn't that often a pilot could spend the entire flight doing aerobatics or, as we called it, turning and burning. Well, that young lady and I did lots of turning and burning that day. Along with loops and aileron rolls, we did immelmanns, Cuban-Eights, barrel-rolls, a split S, and I don't remember what all. I won't describe all these. Suffice it to say that they can be a bit disorienting and conducive to vertigo. Not for her though! She was thriving on all of it. I put more G forces on her young body, not to mention my older body, on that flight than most combat pilots experience during a mission.

I told her that fuel was getting down to where we would have to land shortly. Her response: "I don't want to land—I don't want this to end." *Okay,* I thought, *we'll take it a bit further.*

I asked her if she wanted to experience what a dive-bomb pass felt like. "Oh, yes!" I picked a target on the ground, rolled the jet nearly inverted, and pulled the nose down hard into a steep 45-degree dive. I made a couple of quick adjustments to the flight path to get the gunsight where I wanted it while accelerating to 500 knots. After reaching the point where I would release the bombs, I initiated a gut-wrenching recovery from the dive, followed immediately by a six to seven-G hard turn in one direction, then a hard reversal to the other direction, all designed to avoid anti-aircraft fire. My initial thought was perhaps I had taken it too far with her. But no! Same reaction—"That was so neat, I loved it."

I asked her if she wanted to do some dogfight maneuvers. "Oh, yes!" I told her to imagine we had a bandit on our tail ready to blow us away with missile or cannon. I explained to her what I was going to do and that it would be violent, so she would not be surprised. With that, I did a maximum performance 7 to 8-G break turn to the left, designed to force the bandit to the outside of my flight path. The G suit pressure was tremendous as I held the turn, and I could well imagine the pressure on her small body. I then abruptly shoved the stick full forward to unload the Gs, did a violent reverse turn in the opposite direction, and reapplied the high Gs, all designed to get my gunsight on the bandit for a snapshot with the cannon. Then, another violent unload of G forces and accelerate away. After that, I fully expected her to say, "I've had enough!" But no! Same reaction. She loved it.

With that, we headed back to base for landing. I had given that young lady an incentive flight like no other I have given in my career. And of all the incentive flights I gave, it is the only one I remember fondly. So, you ask, what was the lesson I relearned from that young lady? Simply this: Never, never, judge a person by their appearance.

I was reminded of the Lord's words to the prophet Samuel. God sent Samuel to anoint one of the sons of Jesse as the next king of Israel. Samuel looked at Jesse's seven sons, all of them having the stature and appearance of a king. But the Lord told Samuel that He had not chosen any of them. Samuel asked Jesse if he had other sons, and Jesse told him he had one other, the youngest, the runt of the family who was tending sheep. Samuel said, "Send someone for him." When David arrived, the Lord told Samuel, "This is whom I have chosen. Anoint him." And then the Lord said to Samuel, "Man looks at the outward appearance; the Lord looks on the heart." And the Lord called David, "a man after my own heart."

Well, I had made a snap judgment concerning both my passengers that day—that strong, muscular young man and that little wisp of a gal—based on the outward appearance of each. And I was wrong on both counts. That young lady may have come in a small package, but inside that small package beat a warrior's heart. And I respected that.

We climbed down from the jet, and she was bubbling over. She thanked me again and again for what she said was an experience of a lifetime, and one she would never forget. I, in turn, thanked her for the enjoyment and pleasure I had received from her enjoyment and reactions during the flight. And as we parted, I said something to her that I don't recall ever saying to anyone else to whom I gave incentive flights over the years. I told her, "Young lady, you would make a good fighter pilot." And I meant it!

CHAPTER 27

RANDOM OTHER COMBAT MEMORIES (F-105)

When I reported into the 34th Tactical Fighter Squadron at Korat, Thailand, I was assigned to the flight of one of the majors in the squadron. He was highly thought of by the other pilots, and I considered myself fortunate to have him as my flight commander. Shortly afterward, within a week or so as I recall, he was shot down over North Vietnam. No parachute was observed, and no call was received from him on his survival radio. For two days, fighters in the area called on Guard Channel, trying to get a response from him. There was no response. After two days, he was officially listed as MIA (missing in action). Years later, when the POWs were released, he was not among them. The only rationale conclusion was that he was killed in action or died in captivity.

As the new guy in the squadron and in his flight, I was the one to gather his personal effects from his flight locker. This was where every pilot would stash his personal items before going on a mission, such as billfold, wedding ring, squadron and other identifying patches. The only things we carried with us on a mission were our military identification card and Geneva Convention Card.

As I listed the items in his locker, I went through his billfold to document the amount of money it contained, which was standard procedure. Everything had to be accounted for. His billfold contained pictures of his family. I distinctly remember one picture of a beautiful young lady—his wife—and two of the cutest blonde-haired children who appeared to be from two to four years of age. The thought struck me that that beautiful lady and those two beautiful little children were about to receive some very bad news indeed.

Just prior to this, another pilot in the squadron had to weather abort over the target and returned to base with his six 750 lb. bombs. As I recall, he blew a tire on landing and went off the runway at high speed. As I previously mentioned, the landing speed for the F-105 was very high, and with that bomb load and the other external stores under his wings, his landing speed had to have been around 200 kts. or more. At any rate, the ensuing crash and explosion destroyed the aircraft and killed the pilot. I had barely reported into the squadron, but I had already lost my flight commander over North Vietnam and attended the funeral at the base chapel for another squadron pilot.

On the same day my flight commander was shot down, Colonel David Winn, my class commander during F-105 combat training, was shot down over North Vietnam. Col. Winn was flying out of Takhli, the other F-105 base. Fortunately, the Search and Rescue forces got to him before the North Vietnamese. Col. Winn was a World War II veteran and had flown combat in B-26 Marauders and P-38 Lightnings in that war.

My first combat mission nearly became my last because of a stupid mistake on my part. This was my first flight since leaving the States over a month before, with a side trip to Clark Air Force Base in the Philippines for jungle survival school, so my reflexes were a bit slow and not up to normal speed. In addition to the excitement and knowledge that this was no longer training but the real thing was the fact that AAA sites were reported in the vicinity. All these factors combined to result in my doing exactly what I didn't want to do—screw up.

I rolled in on the target (I forget what it was) at too low an altitude, and by the time I rolled wings level in the dive, I was already at release altitude for the bombs. I should have aborted the pass then and there, but I didn't. Taking a few seconds to maneuver and get the sight on the target put me even lower. Suddenly realizing how low I was, I frantically released the bombs and abruptly yanked back on the control stick to recover from the dive—too abruptly as it turned out. The aircraft shuddered, informing me it was entering a high-speed stall, recovery from which would have been extremely doubtful at that altitude.

The distinct possibility of flying into the ground crossed my mind. I eased up on the back stick pressure, which avoided the stall, and continued to lose altitude while flying a normal 4-G recovery. I finally recovered at an altitude way below normal recovery altitude and way too close to the ground. What an ignominious end that would have been—flying into the ground on the first dive-bomb pass of the first combat mission. I made a vow never to do that again.

I remember the first time I saw red flashes outside the canopy while strafing a convoy of trucks in North Vietnam. I thought probably just the bright sun and its effect on the atmosphere were causing those flashes. I happened to mention it to another pilot, who laughed and informed me that those were anti-aircraft tracer shells going by. The intelligence folks later warned us that that convoy of trucks was probably decoys—damaged or destroyed trucks the North Vietnamese would use as a flak trap for unsuspecting Yankee pilots. It was impossible for the pilot to determine from the air whether those trucks were operational or not. One of our pilots, who apparently didn't get the word, was later shot down and taken prisoner when he was strafing those same trucks.

When strafing a target, it was not advisable to pull out of the dive straight ahead. This made it easier for the gunners to track you. Therefore, a hard turn during recovery was the standard tactic. For some reason, fighter pilots have a natural tendency to make that hard turn to the left. I'm sure there is some biological or psychological reason for this that I don't understand, nor do I care to. Anyway, while strafing a target in Laos one day, I followed the natural tendency and made a high G turn to the left as I recovered from the attack.

A stream of tracer shells immediately greeted me, passing very close to my left. Those gunners weren't dumb. They knew about that tendency for pilots to turn left during recovery. I immediately reversed and made a high G turn to the right. They apparently anticipated this also because I was quickly greeted by another stream of tracer shells passing close inside my right turn. Those gunners were reading my mind. But instead of reversing my turn again back to the left, which they were probably expecting me to do, I rolled out of the turn and pulled up hard and straight ahead. I couldn't see if any tracers were going by behind me. At any rate, I apparently won that little mind game between those gunners and myself since I escaped unscathed.

On May 14, Major Sam Bass, another classmate of mine in F-105 combat training and a squadron mate in the 34th, was killed in a mid-air collision en route to the target. Sam was a prince of a guy, somewhat older than the rest of the pilots, and something of a father figure to the younger pilots.

On May 30, Colonel Phillips was shot down over Laos and rescued. I mentioned before that ejecting over Laos was the worst-case scenario, since the Laotian Communists, the Pathet Lao, allied with the North Vietnamese and Viet Cong, had a reputation of torturing American pilots to death. Relatively few pilots shot down over Laos were rescued. Col. Phillips had come down through the jungle canopy and suffered one broken arm and the dislocation of the opposite shoulder. Despite this, he still managed to contact the rescue folks on his survival radio and communicate his position. The rescue chopper got in and got him out quickly. I still remember that, in the Officers' Club that evening, we pilots had him sitting on a stool and were feeding him beer through a straw while he was swathed in casts from the neck down.

On May 31, another squadron mate, Major Beresik, was shot down over Tiger Island, 15 miles off the coast of North Vietnam, and was killed in action.

As I was walking from the aircraft after landing from a mission one day, the crew chief called for me to come back. He motioned for me to join him underneath the aircraft, whereupon he pointed to a nice size hole in the belly of the jet. Apparently, I had taken a hit without realizing it. We had been doing armed reconnaissance over North Vietnam. I hadn't seen any ground fire, but that was not unusual, and it was common knowledge that, even though you may not see it, you can be fairly certain they are shooting at you. Many pilots were hit or shot down without observing any ground fire.

The location of that hit in the belly of the aircraft was indeed fortunate. Immediately aft of that hole was a steel plate, presumably there for structural strengthening of that section of the fuselage. And just behind that steel plate was the main fuel filter through which all fuel going to the engine passed. Had that steel plate not been there to stop that shell, it would have hit the fuel filter. I would certainly have lost the engine due to flameout, and the entire tail section would have probably been in flames. At any rate, it is certain that if that had been the case, I would have had to eject over North Vietnam.

On June 8, Major Carl Light, another squadron mate, was shot down over North Vietnam after destroying a surface-to-air missile site and while attacking another target. He took a massive hit, and the whole tail section of his aircraft was engulfed in flames. He ejected during the late afternoon and came down in an area containing one of the largest concentrations of anti-aircraft weapons in North Vietnam. Those gun sites prevented the rescue forces from getting to him before nightfall, so he had to spend the night evading and hiding from enemy troops who were conducting a massive search for him.

He told us later that, while he was hiding under the cover of thick shrubs and underbrush, an enemy soldier stepped on his hand. Fortunately, he had the presence of mind to resist the impulse to move his hand. After a short time, the enemy soldier moved on.

Early the next day, contact was reestablished between Carl and the rescue forces, and his identification positively confirmed. Whenever a pilot was not immediately rescued, but had to spend some time on the ground in enemy territory, it was crucial to confirm his identity before commencing the rescue, because of the very real possibility he had been captured, and an English-speaking North Vietnamese was using the pilot's survival radio to direct rescue forces into a flak trap.

Before his combat tour, each pilot submitted to intelligence a list of four questions and answers he alone knew. This was known as his personal identifier and was sealed and kept in the intelligence section. It was opened only if he was shot down and his identity had to be confirmed. The emphasis was to keep those questions simple and the answers one or two words to avoid any confusion or forgetfulness in the heat of battle. This personal identifier would be communicated to the rescue commander, who would question the downed pilot.

Throughout the morning and early afternoon, numerous flights of fighters attacked those gun sites. As I recall, fifty-eight fighter aircraft from various bases were involved in this rescue, which gives the reader some idea of the maximum effort expended to rescue a downed flyer. It was an immense comfort to us pilots, knowing that the rescue forces would move heaven and earth to rescue us. An F-4 engaged in attacking those gun sites was shot down; however, the pilot managed to nurse his crippled jet out over the Gulf of Tonkin before he and his WSO ejected and were promptly rescued.

Finally, in the afternoon, the gun sites had been neutralized to the extent where the rescue helicopter could get in and pick up the downed pilot. And again, it was party time at the Officers' Club when Carl was returned to base.

During another mission, I led a flight of four over an area in North Vietnam where anti-aircraft sites were located. We were searching for them and waiting for them to start firing at us so we could pinpoint their location and attack them. But they weren't cooperating, probably because they suspected our intentions and knew that if they started shooting and gave away their position, they would immediately be on the receiving end of twenty-four 750 lb. bombs. I was frustrated over those gunners' lack of response, and I radioed the others to hold high and keep a lookout while I descended to fly over the area at a lower altitude and slower airspeed. My intention was to tempt those gunners and give them a target they couldn't resist. It didn't work. There was no response, and we finally departed the area. The episode did, however, get me a stern ass-chewing from my Flight Commander, Major Clancy Langford, who had found out about the incident. Clancy was also a good friend. We had gone through F-105 training together. He gave me an order to knock that crap off and stop hanging it out. He made his point clear, although I hadn't done anything others hadn't done. It was a stupid thing for me to do, and I mention it only to emphasize the anger, frustration, and discouragement pilots felt over the political restrictions and rules of engagement that kept us from grinding the enemy into the dust and winning that dirty war in a matter of weeks or less. We could have done it had it not been for the timidity of those political leaders, and our frustration sometimes boiled over and manifested itself in actions a pilot would not normally have considered. More about this in the following chapter.

On June 28, Major Roger Ingvalson, our Squadron Operations Officer, was shot down over North Vietnam. Major Ingvalson was highly respected as a fighter pilot and leader, and well-liked as a person. After he was hit, the aircraft went out of control, and he had to eject at a high airspeed of 500 knots or more. When one has to eject at that speed, it is almost certain serious injuries will be sustained. However, when Rog landed in his chute and checked himself over, he found that he had no injuries whatsoever. He was captured immediately and taken prisoner.

In his deposition, which he wrote when the prisoners were released nearly five years later, Rog said that he took the fact he survived that high speed ejection without injury as a message from the Lord that he would survive whatever followed. And he did! The North Vietnamese kept him in solitary confinement for more than a year and a half. Can you imagine going a year and a half without seeing a friendly face? He was also undergoing physical torture, which the North Vietnamese captors were expert at.

During this time, his wife died. She had suffered from a crippling disease (not sure, but I believe it was muscular dystrophy). His captors simply came to his cell one day and said, "Your wife is dead." In his deposition, Rog said that, when he would dream of his wife and family before that, his wife always showed the effects of that muscular dystrophy, but when she appeared in a dream after he was told she had died, she was in perfect health with no sign whatsoever of that disease.

After the prisoners were released, Rog was reunited with his son, and as I recall, they toured Europe together to get reacquainted. After his retirement from the Air Force as a colonel, he started and managed a very successful Christian prison ministry for quite a few years. He also married the wife of his best friend, another F-105 pilot who had been killed in action. She had also been Roger's first wife's best friend. Their blended families became one.

The term "hero" is used somewhat loosely these days, but in the case of Roger Ingvalson, others I've mentioned, and those I have yet to mention, we are talking about genuine American heroes. Colonel Roger Ingvalson died in December 2011.

Air refueling was conducted on every mission, usually both pre-strike and post-strike refueling. On some missions, after striking the primary target and refueling, the flight would be directed to another target if they had 20mm. cannon ammunition remaining and the target was suitable for strafing. So multiple air-refuelings during a mission were not uncommon. After a short time, air refueling, which to the inexperienced pilot can be a very tense, demanding, and apprehensive experience, became a no-brainer and as normal as breathing for the experienced pilot. That is unless weather or low fuel state was a factor.

After striking the target on one mission, we were headed back to the air-refueling track for post-strike refueling. Our fuel state was lower than normal due to spending a longer time than usual in the target area. Also, it was during the peak of the monsoon season. We were having a difficult time locating the tanker's position due to solid cloud cover and heavy rain, and so we were burning more fuel than a normal join-up would have required. Anyone who has experienced a Southeast Asia monsoon knows what a true monsoon is really like. The rain at times would come down so hard you could barely see your hand in front of your face.

We finally made radar contact with the tanker and were getting within a couple of miles of joining up. But we couldn't maintain a visual sighting because of the thick monsoon clouds and driving rain. We would get a glimpse of the tanker, and then he would disappear again in the clouds. We reduced our overtake speed to the absolute, bare minimum to avoid the very real possibility of a mid-air collision, and slowly, slowly decreased the distance between us using radar. In the meantime, I nervously glanced at my fuel gauge and saw that it indicated a little more than 500 lbs. of fuel remaining. At the rate that J-75 engine burned fuel, I had somewhere around ten minutes before the engine flamed out—that is, assuming the fuel gauge was perfectly accurate. As I recall, the aircraft technical manual stated that the tolerance for accuracy of the fuel quantity gauge was plus or minus 350 lbs. This meant that if the gauge was within tolerance, but on the plus side, I had only 150 lbs. of fuel remaining, and flameout was only a few minutes away.

We closed the distance until radar showed we were five hundred feet or so behind the tanker. The potential for a mid-air collision was definitely a major concern and caused the stress level to max out. And then, there was a momentary thinning of the cloud cover, and we were able to see the tanker and join up with him. I was lowest on fuel, so I would air-refuel first. The other aircraft tucked in close on the tanker's wings to try and keep him in sight. I would take on a minimum amount of fuel at first, then disconnect so that the other aircraft, also very low on fuel, could do the same. After each aircraft had enough fuel to ensure against flameout, we would each hook up again to take on our full scheduled, post-strike offload.

We continued to experience thick cloud cover and driving rain and were barely able to maintain visual reference on the tanker's faint outline. The tanker pilot turned on his exterior lights to assist us, a procedure not recommended in a combat zone, but in the conditions we were facing, it was obvious such a restriction was meaningless.

As I moved into the refueling position, I glanced again at my fuel gauge. It was indicating just slightly above zero fuel remaining. I knew I better get hooked up on the first attempt because I probably didn't have enough fuel for a second attempt. As I nudged the power up and slowly, ever so slowly, moved forward to insert the refueling boom nozzle into the refueling receptacle on the nose of my F-105, I fully expected a sudden silence and loss of thrust due to engine flameout. But it didn't happen, thank God.

I made contact, and fuel began to flow. At times, while I was hanging on to that boom for dear life (no exaggeration), the tanker would disappear momentarily in the thick monsoon clouds and rain. Then suddenly, just before I was going to disconnect to avoid a collision, or there would be damage to the refueling boom, its lights and faint outline would appear again. The pilots of the other aircraft had the same experience. It was, to say the least, a bit intense and scary, but we all managed to stay connected to the refueling boom and get our fuel in turn. And I still distinctly remember the gigantic feeling of relief when I peeked at the fuel gauge and saw that indicator needle start to rise as fuel poured into the tanks. I realized I would not have to eject in the middle of that monsoon storm after all.

On July 1, Lt. Colonel Jack Modica, another classmate of mine during F-105 combat training, was shot down over North Vietnam and rescued. His rescue had some interesting sidelights to it and involved a lieutenant countermanding a general's order. LTC Modica's rescue was coordinated by one of the Misty Fast FACS (forward air controllers) who operated in North Vietnam, and for whom we strike pilots felt a special appreciation because, again, we knew they would go to any extreme to rescue a downed pilot. Also, we liked to work with them because the targets they directed us against were usually of higher value than those selected by the intel folks at higher headquarters.

LTC Modica flew P-38 Lightning fighters during World War II and was a former test pilot. When he ejected from his severely damaged and out of control F-105, he ended up on the ground with serious injuries from that ejection. Basically, he was incapacitated and barely able to move. Nevertheless, using his survival radio, he called in air attacks on nearby enemy forces. The Misty FAC immediately called for rescue forces and emphasized the critical condition of the downed pilot. He called other fighter aircraft in the vicinity to provide air cover against enemy ground forces and defenses and maintained constant surveillance of the downed pilot.

While coordinating all this and waiting for the rescue forces to arrive, the Misty FAC received a radio call advising him that some general at 7th Air Force Headquarters in Saigon had ordered the termination of the rescue attempt because it would interfere with a high priority mission conducted in the general area. The Misty pilot refused to terminate the rescue operation. When told again that the general was ordering him to cease the rescue operation, that Misty pilot, who by the way was a 1st lieutenant, told the person calling that he wanted him to ask that general just what he, Misty, was to tell the downed F-105 pilot on the ground with serious injuries about why they were calling off the rescue attempt and abandoning him to the North Vietnamese. The Misty pilot made it clear that he would not stop the rescue operation until he got an answer from that general.

This undoubtedly caused some fussing and fuming at the headquarters in Saigon; nevertheless, the Misty pilot soon got another call telling him to continue the rescue. He did, and the rescue folks soon got my classmate out of there and prevented him from being taken as a POW. That Misty pilot was later called to Saigon, apparently to explain why he ignored that general's order. But it so happened that the 7th Air Force commander, a four-star general, had a soft spot in his heart for the Misty pilots. He stepped in and, instead of reprimanding that pilot, the four-star praised him for his initiative and aggressiveness in coordinating the rescue of that downed pilot.

It took guts for that Misty pilot, a 1st lieutenant, to countermand that general's order in his determination to rescue that downed pilot, and it speaks highly of the superb quality of those Misty pilots. It was also much appreciated by the rest of us, since it could be one of us on the ground and injured in enemy territory the next day, hoping and praying for rescue.

The accounts of LTC Modica's rescue and the rescue of Major Light, which I previously described, are included in the book *Bury Us Upside Down*, a history of the Misty Forward Air Controller operations in North Vietnam.

There were many dramatic rescues of downed pilots in North Vietnam, and equally dramatic, although not as many, in Laos and South Vietnam. The search and rescue folks, the A-1 "Sandy" pilots who generally coordinated the rescues, and the Jolly Green helicopter crews who extracted the downed pilots, were held in high esteem by the fighter pilots. Their courage, daring, and willingness to "hang it all out" to rescue a downed pilot cannot be overemphasized. Many of them were themselves shot down during rescue operations. The casualty level among the Search and Rescue units was high.

I mentioned that the rescue of LTC Modica had some interesting sidelights to it. Besides the lieutenant countermanding the general's order, another story was of the Pararescue Sgt. Joel Talley who had just arrived in the combat zone for this, his first combat mission. Talley scaled down from the chopper to the ground to get LTC Modica, and he held him on his lap on the tree penetrator seat as they were hoisted back up to the helicopter, all the while under enemy fire. Talk about a dramatic introduction to the war! We heard later that he was awarded the Air Force Cross, the second highest award for valor in combat, for his courage on this mission.

Another interesting sidelight is that LTC Modica kept in contact with his rescuer, Sgt. Joel Talley, and after they both retired from the Air Force, they and their families settled in the same location, in Florida, as I recall. They were neighbors and remained close friends until LTC Jack Modica died on July 4, 2011. As I mentioned previously, friendships made in the military, and especially during combat, have a special bond associated with them, and this was certainly a very special bond.

On August 9, Colonel David Winn, who I mentioned was the class commander of our F-105 combat training class, and who was shot down and rescued on April 15, was shot down again over North Vietnam and this time was taken prisoner. Col. Winn was one outstanding gentleman, officer, fighter pilot, warrior, and leader, and another genuine American hero. I mentioned before that he was a World War II veteran. He had been checked out in nine fighter aircraft and promoted to brigadier general during his career with the USAF and an exchange tour with the Royal Air Force (RAF).

After the release of the POWs, I met Col. Winn at George AFB, where I was an F-4 instructor pilot and the Chief of the Weapons and Tactics Division. There was a base chapel service honoring a group of those returning POWs, and Col. Winn was in that group. He remembered me and our F-105 training days and referred to me as the guy who kept him out of trouble. I'm not sure what he meant by that, and the only thing I can think of is that I helped him plan a cross-country strike mission that was part of the training curriculum.

Part of that honor ceremony for the POWs was a missing man flyby by a flight of four F-4s. I was flying the number three position in the formation, the missing man position. As we came over the chapel in tight formation, I pulled out of the formation, lit the afterburners, and pointed the nose toward heaven. This symbolized our brother flyers who had left us and not returned, who had been killed. It also honored those who had suffered captivity with all the suffering that entailed.

Col. David Winn went to be with his Lord and brother flyers in September 2009.

I remember when I was sitting in a bar in Bangkok drinking strong Asian beer with a fellow F-105 pilot, Captain Richard Allee, another classmate of mine in F-105 training. As I recall, we both were on a few days R&R. I suddenly noticed tears running down his cheeks, and I asked him what the matter was. He said something to the effect that he wasn't going to make it through his combat tour. I tried to shake him out of it by telling him he was just having a case of the jitters, and that, of course, he was going to complete his combat tour—both of us were. He looked me straight in the eyes, and with those tears running down his cheeks, said to me, "I'm telling you, Darrell, I know I'm never going to see my wife and son again."

Not long afterward, close to the end of his combat tour, he was dead. During an attack on a target in Laos, he took major hits, setting the whole rear section of his aircraft ablaze. Apparently, he continued the attack after being hit because his bombs landed square on target. According to another pilot in the flight, there was no attempt to recover from the dive, no ejection attempt, and no Mayday call. After the bomb release, he went straight into the ground with the airplane. The only probable cause that makes any sense is that he must have taken a hit in the cockpit and died immediately after releasing the bombs.

My friend, Captain Richard Allee, received the Air Force Cross posthumously, the second-highest award for valor in combat.

There were other squadron mates shot down during my combat tour in addition to those mentioned. A list of all of them is not my intention. But keep in mind that there were two other F-105 squadrons at Korat in addition to the 34th TFS, as well as the three F-105 squadrons at Takhli. These other five squadrons also had their share of losses.

The Air Force's total buy of F-105s was a little over eight hundred. We lost 395 F-105s during the Vietnam War, nearly half the total inventory. The total number of fighter-type aircraft lost by the Air Force and the Navy and Marines in Vietnam was over 2,500. If helicopter losses are added, the number goes above 10,000. The loss of 58,000 troops, the wounding and maiming of tens of thousands more, the loss of all those aircraft and other resources, the innumerable lives devastated and the agony suffered by so many families, both friendly and enemy, and the utter desolation of villages and countryside stuns the imagination with the horror and waste of it all. All that carnage, devastation, and destruction because of a war that could have been won in a matter of weeks, or at the most months, but was allowed to drag on for nearly ten years because of poor civilian and military leadership at the time. More on that in the following chapter.

In closing this chapter, I'll confess to having guilt feelings ever since I returned from my combat tour, guilt over the fact that others were shot down and I wasn't, although the issue was in doubt at times—guilt over others taken prisoner and suffering terribly at the hands of their captors that I was spared. That guilt remains today and will remain as long as I live. Many may criticize me for this or think I'm some sort of a wacko, but I have discovered that such feelings are common among combat veterans. So I'm pleased to be in good company.

CHAPTER 28

THOUGHTS AND COMMENTS ON WAR

I previously mentioned how the strategy employed during the Vietnam War and the manner in which we fought the war caused great frustration, anger, and demoralization on the part of those fighting it. Not all, but a great many of the targets we struck were of little or no value in forcing the enemy to reconsider his aggression. The high-value targets, the destruction of which would have greatly hurt the enemy, drastically inhibited his capability to continue the war, and quickly brought him to the negotiating table, were kept off-limits by our political authorities.

We were losing aircraft and pilots, as well as thousands of Army and Marine ground casualties, and for what? The United States had the greatest military in the world, and its Soldiers, Sailors, Marines, and Airmen were ready, willing, and able to win that war quickly, decisively, and with minimal casualties. After all, North Vietnam was a third-rate country, weak economically and technologically, and dependent on the Soviet Union for the means to conduct war. Damaging or destroying North Vietnam's infrastructure at a level they were not willing or able to absorb would have quickly ended their support, in both manpower and material, of the Viet Cong insurgency in South Vietnam. And without North Vietnam's support, the Viet Cong insurgency would have rapidly withered on the vine.

The primary factor leading to defeat in Vietnam, other than our strategy that in itself contained fatal flaws, was that many of our political leaders—not all of them, but too many of them at the highest decision levels—lacked the will to win and to do what was necessary to win. After getting us into the war, they failed to follow through with the determination, iron will, and perseverance necessary to see it through to a successful conclusion. And since in our system of government, the military leadership is rightly subject to the authority and decision-making of the civilian political leadership, our military was put in a position of conducting the war with a no-win strategy.

The political leaders were worried that an all-out military offensive against North Vietnam, which would have probably ended the war in a matter of weeks, might cause Russia or China to enter the war. The fact that China had entered the Korean War with substantial forces undoubtedly was a primary cause of this worry. But China and North Vietnam had a long history of enmity toward each other. Also, the Vietnam War's political/military situation was vastly different from that of the Korean War.

During the Korean War, the Chinese understandably considered American forces crossing the 38th parallel into North Korea a threat to their territorial integrity since that would place American forces close to their border. But an invasion of North Vietnam by American ground forces was not seriously considered as an option because of a number of factors, the primary one being that it was unnecessary. An all-out air offensive against prime targets throughout North Vietnam early on would have been sufficient to cripple, if not to destroy, their capability to support the insurgency in South Vietnam. In addition, it would have devastated their economy. That air offensive, without a ground invasion by American and South Vietnamese forces, would not have posed a threat to China's territorial integrity, and to think that China would commit substantial forces to support the insurgency in South Vietnam without such a direct threat was indeed an unrealistic stretch of the political-military imagination. As I said, the situation concerning China during the Vietnam War was far different from that during the Korean War.

As far as Russia was concerned, it supplied the North Vietnamese the vast majority of weapons used against us, including virtually all air defense weapons. Russia used virtually all political and economic means and threats of war to achieve her objectives, but the last thing Russia wanted was war with the United States. In any situation involving a potential confrontation of Russian and American military forces, both Russia and America would desperately seek compromise, evidenced by the outcome of the Cuban missile crisis. Thus, this fear too was politically and militarily unrealistic.

And so, our leaders settled on a strategy of "gradualism"—that is, increasing the pressure on the enemy little by little, being careful not to hurt him too badly and alarm China and Russia, until he finally had enough and cried uncle. I once read that President Johnson, referring to Ho Chi Minh, the elderly communist revolutionary leader of North Vietnam, said that he was going to "touch up" Ho Chi Minh and get him to the negotiating table. In other words, that old third-world communist revolutionary leader was no match for a shrewd, powerful Texas politician who was expert at "touching up" others to get them to do what he wanted.

This attitude was common among the political and military leadership, as well as the military overall. After all, the United States was the strongest military power in the world, and North Vietnam was a backwoods, developing, third-world nation. Forgotten was the fact that Ho Chi Minh, with his Vietminh forces, had defeated the French and ended their colonization. Well, the President was in for a rude awakening. Instead of "touching up" Ho Chi Minh, President Johnson was himself "touched up" and convinced not to run for another term as President.

All this showed an appalling ignorance of the enemy—his history, culture, mindset, patience, cruelty, and radical willingness to suffer tremendous losses for his cause. And so this, combined with our ineffective strategy, set the stage for our eventual failure to achieve our objectives in Vietnam.

When we eventually did mount an air offensive against North Vietnam's infrastructure during the Nixon administration, it was too late. Political and public support for the war had been lost. We forced the North Vietnamese to release our prisoners, thank God. However, the policy of "Vietnamization" was now in progress, that is, training the South Vietnamese forces to take over the conduct of the war, which changed the American role to one of primarily training instead of combat. This was accompanied by a gradual withdrawal of American forces.

Then too, "Watergate" was on the political horizon, which compromised President Nixon's leadership and further eroded political and public support for continued assistance to South Vietnam. Finally, Congress—specifically a Democratic Congress—cut off all funding to the South Vietnamese, which sealed their fate. The North Vietnamese mounted an invasion of South Vietnam in 1975, soon entered Saigon, deposed the South Vietnamese government, and achieved their decades-old objective of uniting the two Vietnams under communism.

In addition to the "know your enemy" lesson mentioned above, another lesson we should have learned long ago from the history of warfare, and.one we had to relearn in Vietnam at great cost, is that "gradualism" is not a strategy for victory but defeat. "Gradualism," in the eyes of one's enemy, denotes weakness, indecision, hesitancy, and an unwillingness to do what it takes to achieve victory. "Gradualism" gives aid and comfort to the enemy, and it will also invariably result in a war of longer duration and more casualties. This was unarguably the case in Vietnam.

General Douglas MacArthur said, "In war, there is no substitute for victory." However, there can be differing definitions of victory. In World War II, victory was the total defeat and unconditional surrender of the Nazi regime in Europe and the military dictatorship in Japan. In Korea, our objective was not the eradication of the North Korean regime, but the defeat of the North Korean invasion of South Korea, the establishment of a democratic government in South Korea, and the development of South Korea into a strong political and military ally of the United States. Were we victorious in Korea? Yes!

The lengthening war and the failure of our political leaders to pursue a winning strategy and get it over with led to the large, vocal, and often violent public peace demonstrations. These not only served to increase the timidity and indecision of our political leaders and further erode the will to win (after all, we're talking about votes here), but also served to give direct aid and comfort to the enemy. And the naïveté and ignorance of those peace demonstrators led to disastrous results.

David Horowitz, who during the Vietnam War was one of the main leaders of the peace movement and who today is one of the main conservative spokesmen, wrote an article (I believe it was in the *Weekly Standard* magazine) in which he claimed that there were two main accomplishments of the peace demonstrations during the Vietnam War. First, they extended the war by four years or so, and second, they caused an additional thousands upon thousands of casualties of both friendly and enemy forces. And he said that if the casualties of Cambodia were added to that number of additional casualties caused by the peace protestors and the politicians who caved into them, then the number is probably over two million. That's because, after our withdrawal, the Khmer Rouge immediately instituted a program of genocide in which an estimated 1.5 million Cambodians were brutally murdered. Horowitz, by the way, bases his rationale for these two disastrous results of the peace demonstrations—the extension of the war and the horrendous increase in casualties—on the writings of General Giap, the Supreme Commander of the North Vietnamese military. General

Giap stated in his writings that, by the end of 1968, the Politburo of North Vietnam, realizing that they could never defeat the United States military and given the horrendous losses they were suffering and which they could no longer absorb, decided to halt the war, wait ten years or so, and then try again to take over South Vietnam.

But then, the violent peace demonstrations in the United States became widespread, along with the Democratic National Convention violence in late 1968. General Giap said this made the North Vietnamese leadership realize they didn't have to defeat the American military; all they had to do was hang on and keep fighting. The American public, along with many of their politicians, would bring about America's defeat. And they were right.

It sickens me when I read about or see on television some aging peacenik bragging about their ending the Vietnam War. What is especially sickening is their appalling ignorance of, or their deliberate rejection of, the historical facts that clearly identify the disastrous consequences and the immeasurable suffering that were the fruits of their so-called peace movement.

As I write this, decades later, our nation has been involved in a war against radical Islamic terrorism for over 18 years. Our military has been heavily engaged in combat operations in both Iraq and Afghanistan, as well as in operations in Syria and other areas of the Middle East. Although the terrorist forces of Al-Qaeda, the Taliban, and ISIS have been seriously decimated, and the majority of our military forces withdrawn from Iraq and Afghanistan, the war against terror is by no means over. And I have a feeling that many of our politicians, as well as a good share of the American public, are repeating the same mistakes made during the Vietnam War.

Americans, by nature, are a people who like to get things done. If there is a problem, solve it! If there is a need, fill it! If there is an opportunity, go for it! This attitude, in large measure, has enabled America to become the most powerful, the most affluent, the most free, the most benevolent, and the most generous nation in history.

But it is also a major cause of frustration when expected results do not materialize within a reasonable period of time, or an effort is required that extends beyond the foreseeable future. Americans must realize that the war against terror, due to its nature and the nature of the enemy, is different from any other and requires a commitment for the long haul. The consequences the United States suffered in losing the war in Vietnam will pale in comparison to the consequences the nation will suffer if we lose the war against terrorism.

The loss of Vietnam, from a strategic standpoint, did not measurably affect the nation's balance of power in the world. Nor did it adversely affect the average American's living standards or way of life. Losing the war against terrorism, however, or not winning it decisively and unambiguously, will greatly diminish America's superpower standing and influence in the world, embolden more and more terrorist attacks against Americans at home and abroad, reduce both the actual security and the perception of security on the part of the population, and result in ever-increasing and tighter monitoring and controls on peoples' activities in an attempt to provide the level of security the people demand. And this, in turn, will result in a significant deterioration in what is known, and too often taken for granted, as the American way of life.

In my following comments, I am speaking of the radical jihadist Islamists and not the peaceful Muslim nations who are themselves threatened by the radical jihadists.

I fear that, just as many of our leaders and citizens failed to understand the nature of our enemy during the Vietnam War, so today, many fail to understand the nature of the terrorist enemy we now face. It is a common failing of not only Americans, but in general of all Western peoples, to assume that people of other cultures, although different in many ways, basically think as we do with the same rationale and logic, and that agreement, although it may be extremely difficult and time-consuming to achieve, can always be reached through diplomacy. Therefore, hostile action can always be avoided through negotiation and compromise based on shared rationale and logic and mutual self-interests. This can be a dangerous assumption. Pearl Harbor should have cured us of that assumption.

The war against terrorism will have its lulls and its swells, but I doubt the time will ever come when we can truly say, "it is over." The 9/11 terrorist attack on America was the beginning of a new era.

The terrorist enemy considers negotiation not as a means to reach a compromise and a peaceful resolution acceptable to all, but simply as another weapon to deceive and weaken their opponent, delay any forceful action by their opponent, and thereby give themselves more time and opportunity to achieve their goals and objectives.

The terrorist enemy respects and responds to only one thing— force and power. And the sooner the Western nations, as well as all other nations desiring peace, fully realize the nature of the enemy and the nature of the conflict, the sooner they will be able to collectively marshal the will, power, unity, and resources necessary to win the war against terrorism. And winning will entail either totally destroying the terrorist enemy, their means of support, and the evil of their radical ideology and methods, or convince them that they cannot possibly win their religious war and clash of civilizations and that the only way to avoid their own destruction is to renounce terrorism and engage in good faith negotiations for a peaceful resolution.

All war is political in nature. As Clausewitz, a Prussian officer and author of works on military strategy, said, "War is a continuation of politics by other means." The problem, however, arises when a nation is at war and that war is politicized, that is when the war is used by an opposing political party or entity to gain political advantage—in other words, when the war is used as a tool to gain political power.

This was precisely the situation that existed, and to some extent, continues to exist with our going to war in Iraq, although the majority of American troops have since been withdrawn.

As the war dragged on with casualties and the drain on resources, the Democratic Party leadership criticized and condemned President Bush and the Republican Party for invading Iraq. This was a clear example of blatant hypocrisy and sewer politics, since many of those Democratic leaders doing the criticizing, including a former Vice President, and a lady Senator and future Secretary of State and Presidential candidate, were adamant in recommending going to war. They voted to authorize going to war, with the primary objective being to depose the brutal and genocidal dictator Saddam Hussein in order to prevent his use of weapons of mass destruction, which the intelligence agencies of every major western nation, as well as some Middle East nations, said he had and that he had said he would use them.

The secondary objective of the war in Iraq, as well as for Afghanistan, where America and NATO were also at war, was to replace their regimes, where political, economic, and social conditions were fertile ground for terrorists and terrorism to thrive, with some form of democratic government. With the hindsight of time, it has become clear that replacing a tyranny with a democracy can be extremely difficult since a dictatorship is all many of those people have known for centuries. In my opinion, it would be best in some cases to replace a cruel tyrant with a benevolent dictator, if there is such a person, one who possesses integrity and who puts the needs and welfare of the people first, rather than imposing upon the people the considerable responsibilities associated with a democratic form of government they are neither able nor willing to accept.

It is not my intent in this narrative to justify the decision to go to war in Iraq. But I will say that, given the hostile words and acts of Saddam Hussein, the preponderance of intelligence confirming that he had weapons of mass destruction, and the wide agreement among our political and military leaders, as well as those of other countries that his regime posed a clear and present danger, it is difficult to justify a decision not to go to war.

Were mistakes made? Of course! In all wars, mistakes are made. Anyone who has been involved in the development of war plans, which I was during my staff tour at a NATO headquarters, can attest to the fact that every plan contains shortcomings and that some of the intelligence on which those plans are based will probably be proven faulty once the plan is implemented.

The complexities and confusion—the fog surrounding war and the conditions leading to war—virtually eliminate the possibility of perfect intelligence and perfect planning. That is why plans are continually reviewed, the situation and conditions reassessed, and strategy and tactics revised as necessary to achieve objectives. Nevertheless, planners and policymakers must act on the best intelligence available to them at the time, and this is what President Bush did. To fail to do so is a dereliction of duty.

When politicians, talking heads, the media, and bloggers criticize policymakers who acted on the best intelligence available at the time, and especially when they who are doing the criticizing accepted that intelligence as valid and demanded strong action based on that intelligence, they are engaging in blatant hypocrisy and gutter partisan politics. And that reflects a lack of integrity, honesty, principle, and honor.

Certainly, mistakes and misjudgments made in the planning and conduct of a war must be identified to avoid repetition and determine accountability. But the time to do that is not during the conflict, but afterward. While our troops are at war, it is absolutely crucial that the war not be politicized as a tool to gain political power, but that everyone, from political and military leaders to the public, not air the dirty laundry for the world to see, but present a united front that communicates to the enemy an iron will and determination to, in the words of President Kennedy, "bear any burden" to achieve victory. The requirement not to politicize the war was violated numerous times during the wars in both Vietnam and Iraq.

There are too many in positions of power who give lip service to bipartisanship and to the aforementioned honorable character traits, but their actions reflect a cynicism and lust for power that take priority over these noble character traits. Our Founding Fathers clearly realized that in a Democratic Republic, which is what they gave us, two things were absolutely mandatory: 1. That the nation be established on the foundation of Judeo-Christianity, since it is only on those principles and standards that a free and democratic society can thrive and prosper; and 2. That since the citizens choose their leaders, they must be informed and knowledgeable concerning candidates for high office. Time and time again, they warned the people to be very, very careful to elect persons of faith, virtue, honesty, and honor, and never, never to elect a person to high office who had a lust for power. As I recall, Washington warned against this in his final address upon leaving office.

Our Founders made our government representatives directly responsible to the people in establishing our republican form of government. They also emphasized the need for the members of our three branches of government to use the common sense and wisdom God gave them, to seek His guidance in directing the affairs of the nation, and always, always, to put the welfare and best interests of the country and the people ahead of partisan politics. During any administration, it is the primary duty of the political opposition to develop well thought out, reasonable, and realistic changes to policies and legislation to enhance the nation's military, economic, social, and international posture. Notice that the operative words here are "well thought out," "reasonable," and "realistic."

Too often, policies and legislation offered by the political opposition lack those operative words and reflect instead a lust for power, an emphasis on partisan politics instead of the common welfare, and a priority of satisfying the needs of their special interests and contributors instead of the needs of the country. This is not only dangerous during peacetime but can have disastrous consequences during wartime as referenced in the above. In my opinion, it comes dangerously close to the threshold of treason.

A final word on my personal philosophy of war and peace. I believe, as individuals, we should strive to live according to the Ten Commandments and the New Testament rules that Jesus gave in his Sermon on the Mount, including His command: "Love the Lord your God with all your heart and mind and soul and strength; and "Love your neighbor as yourself." But when, as a people and a nation, we are attacked or forced into war, I believe Old Testament rules apply of using whatever force is necessary to quickly and decisively defeat the enemy, giving no quarter or respite until victory is achieved. That is the most effective strategy for restoring peace and justice in the shortest possible time and with the fewest casualties.

We must combat evil with good, and this oftentimes requires going to war. A fact of life, the logic and truth of which the radical progressive liberals, the moral relativists, and the secular humanists among us seem incapable of grasping, is that any compromise with evil invariably leads to evil overtaking the good. There is no moral equivalency between evil and good, and as history proves, compromising with evil is a sure path to corruption, confusion, chaos, and eventually, total disaster.

I thank the reader for bearing with me as I shared my opinions and judgments concerning the Vietnam War and the War on Terrorism and the obligations of our political leaders. Perhaps you agree with me; perhaps you don't. But after twenty-six and a half years of service as a Marine and Air Force officer and fighter pilot, I felt both obliged and entitled to make it clear where I stand and why I feel as I do.

CHAPTER 29

LAST MILITARY FLIGHT (F-4)

I t has been said that there are only two really bad days for a fighter pilot. One of those bad days is the one when the fighter pilot straps on the jet, knowing it is his last flight. The other bad day is the one when the fighter pilot straps on the jet, not knowing it is his last flight.

The good Lord had spared me from that "not-knowing" bad day over a twenty-four-year military flying career, although He had allowed me to come close to experiencing it a number of times. But finally, just as every fighter pilot who survives a military flying career eventually experiences that "knowing" bad day, so my time had arrived to do likewise. The day had come for me to strap on the jet, knowing that it was my final flight as a command pilot in a military jet fighter.

I had submitted the paperwork for my retirement from the Air Force. I made that decision after I was notified I would be receiving orders sending me to a headquarters staff position. Knowing that, given my age (I had reached the half-century mark), I would never get back into the cockpit again, combined with the fact that I had joined the Air Force for the sole purpose of flying as a military aviator, I decided it was time to call it a career. I had accumulated over four thousand hours of flying time, virtually all of it in jet fighters, had flown combat, and had had a good many unique, memorable, and—yes, a few terrifying experiences to look back on and remember.

But far more important than remembering those experiences is remembering those individuals with whom I shared those experiences. For all those years, I had the great privilege of being a part of the fighter pilot community. There is a bonding that takes place between those who fly fighter aircraft that is unique and special, a type of bonding that most people will never experience in a lifetime. It is true that extremely close bonding is common in all the military branches, especially the combat units, and is most prevalent among such elite units as the Green Berets, the Rangers, the Marine Recon, Seals, Submariners, etc. This bonding is strengthened during wartime by the very real presence of danger and the distinct possibility of being maimed or killed.

The bonding within the fighter pilot community seems amplified to some extent. I'm sure many can describe this bonding and the reasons for it far better than I; nevertheless, in my limited capability for expression, I will try. First, I would attribute it to the fact that the fighter pilot community is only a very minuscule segment of the military community as a whole, not to mention the rest of the country's population, and therefore it is one of the most elite of communities, whether military or civilian. Second, I would attribute it to the extreme pressures and demands of training not only to get those wings, but to keep them, and the extreme competitiveness of the profession. Third, I would attribute it to the fact that the fighter pilot is master of one of the most complicated and sophisticated marvels of modern aeronautical engineering and computer technology, and is expert in using that marvel as a weapon of war. Fourth, I would attribute it to the dangers inherent in the intense and violent flying fighter pilots normally engage in while in close proximity to each other and to the ground. At times, they must take that jet to the very edge of, or even a little beyond, its design performance limits. And fifth, I would attribute it to the fact that, not only in wartime but also in peacetime, whenever the pilot straps on the jet, that very real presence of danger and the possibility of not coming back is always there and is a major part of the aura that makes the fighter pilot's life so intriguing. In short, the fighter pilot courts death on a daily basis. The cockpit of a fighter aircraft is a place of self-discovery where one is faced with the stark reality of one's capabilities and limitations. It is a place where one feels more alive than at any other time. Add to all this the fact that the fighter pilot sees things few others see, does things few others do, and goes where few others go, and one can perhaps gain at least a partial understanding of the bonding inherent in the fighter pilot's profession.

This bonding remains even after one's flying career has ended. As an example, take two former fighter pilots who flew together in the same squadron long ago, who haven't seen each other for years and who bump into each other one day. They will invariably revert to their flying days, recounting the experiences they shared, probably over a couple of beers, and it will be as if the intervening years had never passed. They may mention those intervening years and their current professions in a cursory fashion; however, the focus of their conversation and remembrance will most likely be their military flying days together.

Another evidence of this bonding is that when fighter pilots remember or think of their brother fliers, they tend to remember and think of them as they were during their squadron days together. Even if they have seen firsthand the effects of time, age, or sickness on a former fellow aviator, when they think about their shared experiences and visualize him in their mind, they visualize him as he was those many years ago—young, vibrant, intense, and perhaps a little crazy.

Enough of all that and back to my final flight as a military aviator. My final flight was quite appropriate, and indeed even ironic, considering my impending retirement. I was scheduled, along with another pilot who was also retiring, to deliver two F-4 Phantoms to the Air Force Storage and Reclamation Facility at Davis-Monthan Air Force Base in Tucson, Arizona.

The Storage and Reclamation Facility, commonly referred to as the Boneyard, is where the Air Force and Navy aircraft being retired from the active inventory are taken to be chopped up for salvage, stripped for spare parts, or sealed up and stored for possible return to active flying status in the future. The irony of two pilots who would shortly retire delivering two F-4 Phantom jets that were being retired was not lost on us.

We flew the jets from Homestead Air Force Base, Florida, to Ellington Air National Guard Base in Houston, Texas, for refueling, and then on to Davis-Monthan in Tucson. We landed and taxied to the maintenance area where they prepared the jets for storage. As I recall, we declared both jets as Code One—that is, no maintenance problems during the flight.

I had brought a bottle of champagne and some silver goblets I had bought in Spain years before. As I unloaded my luggage from the travel pod, I retrieved that champagne and the goblets. Popping the cork and filling the goblets, the other pilot and I, along with our WSOs, toasted the jets, toasted each other, and with gratitude, toasted our respective flying careers. And with that, my fighter pilot days came to an end.

CHAPTER 30

EPILOGUE

Give me what I had but which is now gone,
The fighter pilot's life and the warrior's special bond.

With the sky my arena, so infinite and vast,
From peaceful tranquility into violence be cast.

God my shelter and shield, against danger to hedge,
Death hovers close when life is lived on the edge.

Stick and throttle and the cockpit as home,
With power undreamt of, which only few have known.

Sleek, fast and deadly, a craft like no other,
Cruel as a mistress and demanding as a lover.

The bond between man and aircraft emotions did cover,
Cursing it as foe, but with the affection of a brother.

Hands trained for battle and mind geared for war,
Man and machine into combat did soar.

And when it's all over, the stories are told,
Getting better and better as the tellers grow old.

Though the body may tire, the march of time has not won,
For the fighter pilot's spirit remains forever young.

~ Darrell Aherns

After retirement from the Air Force, I was a high school teacher for some years in the Phoenix area. As Chairman of the school's Aerospace Science Department, the Air Force Junior Reserve Officer's Training Course (AFJROTC), I taught classes in aviation history, aerodynamics, aircraft design, navigation, space technology, and so forth, as well as classes in global studies and leadership. After a long military career in both the Marines and Air Force, and with the discipline, structure, respect, and motivation all that entailed, the high school environment was a culture shock, to put it mildly.

The curriculum included not only academics in the classroom, but numerous after-school and weekend extra-curricular activities, such as drill competitions, field trips, and numerous community service events. It didn't take me long to discover a few things. One was that, for many of the students, the ROTC classroom was a home away from home. Both dad and mom worked, and the students were basically on their own after school. Second, although they would gripe at times about the discipline, dress, and grooming regulations, and our insistence on responsibility, integrity, honesty, and respectful behavior toward both teachers and fellow students, the vast majority of them inwardly wanted that discipline and those boundaries on their speech, behavior, and appearance. I am convinced it provided them some sense of security. The overwhelming majority wore the uniform with pride because it identified them as someone special.

Third, I had many students with serious problems at home. Many had parents who were divorced, and they couldn't get along with dad's girlfriend or mom's boyfriend. It didn't take my assistants and me long to realize we were surrogate parents to many of these kids. The students knew my office door was always open to them, and on many occasions, I would have a student walk in and ask if they could talk to me. I heard some things that made me want to go find some parents and give them a good, swift kick in the rear.

After getting an earful, I would ask the student if they would mind if I prayed for them. The ACLU and many school authorities would go bonkers over that, but I can truly say I never had a student who said they didn't want me to pray for them. On the contrary, they seemed to appreciate it and often thanked me.

And fourth, I was amazed to discover that many students, including juniors and seniors, were close to being virtually illiterate. They couldn't structure a sentence or a paragraph, couldn't punctuate or spell, had a difficult time reading, were largely ignorant of our country's history, government, and geography—not to mention world geography, and they couldn't work a simple percentage problem. You know there's a problem when you ask a student who was President of the United States in World War II, and they answer John Kennedy. The bottom line was I realized that, in many respects, our public education system in the U.S. had been in freefall the past few decades or so. It was severely diminished from what our Founding Fathers had intended it to be, and what it had been as recently as the 1950s, where it had emphasized both the basics and the liberal arts, which are essential for a well-rounded education.

At the same time I was teaching, I was taking courses for a second master's degree at Fuller Theological Seminary. During the last few years of my military career, I had felt a strong leading to attend seminary. So, for ten years, I took courses one or two at a time at the seminary's Phoenix campus, and then during summer, I spent a month or more at the seminary's home campus in Pasadena, California. I finally completed all course requirements and was awarded the Master of Divinity Degree. Shortly after graduation from seminary, I retired from high school teaching and accepted a call to pastor a local start-up church.

I believe that, as the Bible passage says, "the steps of a man are ordered by the Lord." As I look back over the years, I can see how the three professions that constituted the bulk of my work career were identified early on without my realizing it. As I mentioned in the introduction to this book, my desire to fly and be a fighter pilot goes back to when I was six or seven years old. Then, in my early teens, I experienced a strong leading and desire for preaching and the ministry. Finally, after high school, I entered a Christian teacher's college with the intent to enter the teaching profession.

These three areas—flying, teaching, and ministry—turned out to be, respectively, the arenas of my professional life over a period of more than forty-five years. And it seems that without my being aware of it, each of these areas had been identified as a part of my future by the time I was seventeen years old.

As I approached retirement from the military, I wondered how I would react to it. The experience of my older brother gave me cause for concern. He had joined the Navy a couple of years out of high school and retired after a thirty-year career. The education and vast experience he had gained as a Navy Seabee in the construction of everything from runways and port facilities to housing and schools, as well as in contracting, logistics, and public works management, made him a prime candidate for employment by both government and private contracting agencies. He spent some time as a consultant and member of a study group contracted to determine public works requirements for a county of California over the next twenty-five years. Yet it was clear to those who knew him well that his heart was never completely in it. For thirty years, the Navy had been his profession, his mission, his identity—in short, his life. He seemed lost as a civilian in search of a new identity, a new mission.

His experience caused me some concern as I approached my own retirement from the military. I'm sure a similar concern is felt by anyone who retires from a profession they have long been identified with and engaged in. Nevertheless, I think it is felt more deeply by retired military. And I think this is partly due to the bonding I mentioned previously, the warrior mentality, the nature of the mission, and the attitude of dedication and sacrifice inherent in the code of duty, honor, and country.

At any rate, I wondered how I would adjust to a new identity after more than twenty-six years of having the identities of "Marine" and "Air Force fighter pilot." As it turned out, adjusting to the teaching profession, while at the same time being deeply involved in seminary studies, didn't leave much time to dwell on it, which was a good thing. And after I started preaching, I was surprised to discover that preparing and delivering a sermon, if done with zeal, involved an excitement, passion, and sense of accomplishment similar to that of preparing for a complicated mission and then flying it.

I also discovered that those twenty-six years of military life, my travel to approximately forty countries, living twelve years overseas, experiencing a variety of cultures and traditions, and experiencing combat enabled me on occasions to relate from personal experience and testimony the application of God's Word to peoples' lives in the here and now. I continue to be surprised how effective personal testimony, given humbly and with all honor to God, can be in helping people to see the critical relevancy of God's Word to their lives—past, present, and future—and how it applies to their current circumstances. When people humbly and sincerely relate through personal experience how God's Word helped them to overcome dire circumstances in their own lives, it can be a powerful tool to enable other people to see how God's Word can help them to overcome similar or even different, dire circumstances in their own lives.

Another discovery I made was that many of the attributes that make a good Marine or fighter pilot or any military professional are attributes that make a good preacher and vice versa.

Finally, I discovered the truth of the sayings, "Once a Marine, always a Marine," and "Once a fighter pilot, always a fighter pilot." Even though after retirement, I was, to a great extent, overwhelmed with my teaching duties and seminary studies, I would often revert to my active duty and flying days, reliving in memory some of the experiences mentioned in this book, as well as many others. I can now see that, in addition to just a normal remembering of the past, there was another element involved to some degree—a hesitancy or refusal to admit it was over, or to put it another way, a refusal to cut the cord and press on. Teaching ROTC actually assisted me in this refusal to cut the cord since I was teaching a curriculum primarily consisting of military history and aviation technology, not to mention the opportunities I had to supplement the texts with personal stories and perhaps embellish them just a tiny bit (which I never did.)

Then one day, an incident occurred that clearly impressed on me the fact it was over. I was in Tucson and decided to visit the Air Force Storage and Reclamation Center—the facility mentioned previously where the military stores the aircraft retired from active duty, either keeping them in flying condition, using them for spare parts, or cutting them up for scrap metal. As I drove down the perimeter road viewing the row upon row of hundreds, if not thousands, of aircraft of different types and models, I passed an area that caused me to do a double-take. I stopped and parked alongside the road to take in the view and digest its meaning to me.

In a relatively small area, there sat the hulk of an F-105, while next to it were the remains of an F-100. Close to those were the cut-up sections of an RF-84 and an F-102. And a short distance from those hulks, there was a row of F-4s. I was struck by the fact that in that small, compact area were the five fighter aircraft I had flown and known like the back of my hand, four of them in various stages of destruction, and one of them (the F-4) still intact.

Then the realization dawned on me. Those aircraft had once been the front-line fighters, the apex of technology, speed, and performance, the point of the spear so to speak, the war machines of their day. If they could talk, what amazing stories they could tell. But their days of glory had come and gone, and they had been replaced by more advanced machines of even greater capability and performance.

I realized that, like those aircraft I had flown, my days had come and gone. My days of experiencing the unique joy and ecstasy, the fear and terror, the intensity and adventure of the fighter pilot's life had come and gone, gone forever. And it was time to come to grips with that fact. It was time, as the Apostle Paul put it, "to leave in the past those things which are behind, and reach forward to those things which are ahead."

And so, this I try to do. But in all honesty, I must admit, Lord, help me, that I still miss it so.

CPSIA information can be obtained
at www.ICGtesting.com
Printed in the USA
BVHW051240070421
604337BV00009B/1780

9 781629 671888